GOOD $ENSE

IMPLEMENTATION GUIDE

A Step-by-Step Strategy for Your Church

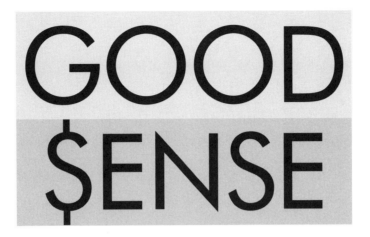

IMPLEMENTATION GUIDE

A Step-by-Step Strategy for Your Church

Dick Towner
With contributions from the
Good $ense Ministry team of
Willow Creek Community Church

GRAND RAPIDS, MICHIGAN 49530

Good $ense Implementation Guide
Copyright © 2002 by Willow Creek Community Church

Requests for information should be addressed to:

Willow Creek Association
67 E. Algonquin Road
Barrington, IL 60010

Zondervan
5300 Patterson SE
Grand Rapids, MI 49530

ISBN: 0-744-13725-X

All Scripture quotations, unless otherwise indicated, are taken from the Holy *Bible: New International Version*®. NIV®. Copyright © 1973, 1978, 1984 by International Bible Society. Used by permission of Zondervan. All rights reserved.

Scripture quotations marked (NLT) are taken from the *Holy Bible,* New Living Translation, copyright © 1996. Used by permission of Tyndale House Publishers, Inc., Wheaton, IL 60189. All rights reserved.

Scripture quotations marked (MSG) are taken from *The Message: The New Testament in Contemporary English*. Copyright 1993 by Eugene H. Peterson. Used by permission of NavPress, Colorado Springs, Colorado, 80935. All rights reserved.

All rights reserved. No part of this publication may be reproduced, stored in a retrieval system, or transmitted in any form or by any means—electronic, mechanical, photocopy, recording, or any other—except for brief quotations in printed reviews, without the prior permission of the publisher.

Cover design by Rick Devon, Adam Beasley

Interior design by Ann Gjeldum

Produced with the assistance of The Livingstone Corporation. Project staff includes: Ashley Taylor, Christopher D. Hudson, and Carol Barnstable.

Printed in the United States of America

03 04 05 06 07/ / 10 9 8 7 6 5 4 3 2

DEDICATION

To Pop and Gram Wernicke who raised me and modeled for me a simple and frugal lifestyle. While their lifestyle was shaped in part by income circumstances, it was lived with contentment, making it easy for me to later accept the biblical truth that a person's life does not consist in the abundance of their possessions.

To my incredibly gifted and incredibly loving wife, Sibyl, who helped me to understand that frugality for its own sake simply leads to sinful hoarding, but that the true end result of frugality is liberality. Thank you, dear Sibyl, for modeling this for me and for helping me to experience the joy of giving.

And finally, to the body of believers known as College Hill Presbyterian Church in Cincinnati, Ohio. Not only did you baptize me as a child, nurture me as a teenager, marry me as a young adult, mature my faith, ordain me as an elder, and allow me to serve as part of the ministerial team for fourteen years, but you encouraged and provided the platform for the development of the vast majority of what is contained within these pages. My gratitude is beyond expression.

CONTENTS

   Foreword 9
   Acknowledgments 11
   Preface 13
1. Foundations of the Good $ense Ministry Movement 15
2. The Implementation Process 19
3. Phase 1: Commitment .23
4. Phase 2: Development .37
5. Phase 3: Launch 49
6. Phase 4: Expansion 59
   Appendix 69

FOREWORD

In school they tell us we're being equipped to earn it. Then for the rest of our lives—for about fifty or sixty hours a week—we're busy making it. We invest countless hours in thought and discussion deciding how to deal with it. We walk around shopping malls for hours on end determining how we're going to spend it. We're caught up more often than we'd like to admit worrying we won't have enough of it. We dream and scheme to figure out ways to acquire more of it.

Arguments over it are a leading cause for marital disintegration. Despair over losing it has even led to suicide. Passion for it causes much of society's crime. The absence of it causes many of society's nightmares. Some view it the root of all evil, while others think of it as the means for great good.

One thing is clear: We cannot afford to ignore the reality of the importance of *money*.

Over the years at Willow Creek Community Church we've been committed to tackling every important issue that faces the people who attend—from nutrition to sexuality, from building character to deepening relationships, from discovering and adoring the identity of God to preparing for death and eternity. One topic, however, that we've learned we must address regularly and directly is the subject that Christians wrestle with almost every day—the issue of how we handle personal finances.

Thankfully, there's no shortage of information on this crucial matter in the Bible, and it provides the basis for the materials you're about to dive into. More than two thousand Scripture passages touch on the theme of money. Jesus spoke about it frequently. About two-thirds of Jesus' parables make reference to our use of financial resources. He once warned that "where your treasure is, there your heart will be also." He talked often about these matters because he understood what was at stake. He knew that, left to our own devices, this area would quickly become a source of pain and frustration—and sometimes bondage. Worse, he saw how easily our hearts would be led astray from pure devotion to God into areas of worry and even obsession over possessions. He wanted to protect us from these pitfalls and to show us the liberty that comes from following him fully in every area of life, including this one.

So get ready to join the ranks of thousands of people from our church and other churches who have received tangible help in this area through *Good $ense.* This vital ministry has been refined and proven over many years by my friend and trusted co-laborer, Dick Towner, along with his Good $ense Ministry team. I'm confident you'll find fresh avenues to increased financial freedom and, along the way, grow a more grateful spirit and generous heart.

And as you and others from your congregation experience this, your church will be liberated so it can reflect more and more of that giving spirit and heart to the community around you, making it a magnet to people who are desperately looking for the kind of freedom, life, and love they see in you.

Bill Hybels
Founding and Senior Pastor
Willow Creek Community Church

ACKNOWLEDGMENTS

There are literally hundreds of people at Willow Creek Community Church and the Willow Creek Association whose expertise, support, wide array of contributions and encouragement were crucial throughout the development and completion of this project. Though space limitations prohibit naming all of them, their ranks include the following:

- The early group of volunteers and staff member George Lindholm who responded to God's vision in 1985 and began the Good $ense Ministry. Their leadership ranks included Warren Beach, Bill and Loretta Gaunt, John Frederick, Chuck Keenon, Jim Kinney, and Carl Tielsch. Stalwarts of the early counseling team included Bill and Joann Allen, Bob Baker, Candy Borst, Barry Gardner, Don and Zona Hackman, Dan Hollerick, Charlie Maxwell, Elizabeth Maring, Tom Stevens, Cyndy Sutherland, and Carol White. Staff assistance in the early years also came from Bruce Bugbee and Ken Fillipini.

- Current Good $ense volunteers, especially the following who have played an active role in the development of the materials: Russ Haan, Jerry Wiseman, Steve Sherbondy, Jenifer Nordeen-Lugar, Dan Rotter and Sue Drake. Thank you for your creativity and passion and the many contributions you made. Thanks, too, to the volunteer Good $ense Ministry Board, not only for your wise counsel and direction over the years, but even more for the deep bonds of friendship and mutual call to ministry we have shared.

- John Tofilon, whom God touched in a special way to become deeply involved in the *Good $ense Budget Course* and whose commitment to this project can only be characterized as "above and beyond." Your contribution has been huge and your life has touched mine.

- Norm Vander Wel and Jon Kopke, two friends of the heart who, though not connected with Willow Creek, provided insight and creativity and encouragement that was exceedingly helpful.

- Jim Riley, who followed me as director of the Good $ense Ministry at Willow Creek Community Church, and has been a true companion of the heart in seeking to help folks understand and implement biblical principles of stewardship in their lives. Thank you, Jim, for your commitment to this project and for your deep friendship.

- Wendy Seidman and her team—Bridget Purdome, Sue Drake, and Rebecca Adler. Their expertise in instructional design makes these materials effective in training and equipping people. Thanks to each of you not only for sharing your expertise but also for taking the core values of this project into your own hearts.

- Christine M. Anderson, who managed the project, interjected her insights and wisdom at all the right times, provided encouragement when it was most needed, and exhibited amazing patience as we worked and reworked and reworked the material.

- Bob Gustafson, Steve Pederson, and Sharon Sherbondy for their expertise and enthusiasm in creating video segments that not only teach and train but also touch the heart.

- Bill Hybels, senior pastor. Early in his ministry, Bill recognized and affirmed the vital connection between a biblical understanding of material possessions and one's spiritual well being. Over the years, his commitment to regular, passionate teaching on this topic has been an invaluable support and encouragement to the Good $ense Ministry . . . and a significant contribution to its effectiveness.

- Jim Mellado, Sharon Swing, and the entire Willow Creek Association Leadership Team for catching the vision for this project and for their support and encouragement as we worked to realize that vision.

- Joe Sherman and the publishing and marketing team at the Willow Creek Association for providing the resources to produce this curriculum and for believing it can make a difference in so many lives.

- Several donors whose faith in this project and generous financial contributions not only provided initial funding but were also a great encouragement to me personally.

PREFACE

Welcome the Good $ense Ministry!

There is a tremendous need for churches today to educate and assist people with managing their resources in God-honoring ways. A Good $ense Ministry does that—it can relieve the crushing stress and anxiety caused by consumer debt, restore marriages torn by the conflict over money, and heal the wounded self-esteem and shattered confidence resulting from poor financial decisions. A Good $ense Ministry helps church leadership to become more comfortable teaching in the church about the once taboo topic of money. A Good $ense Ministry also helps the church itself as people become free to give to God's work.

Most significantly, however, a Good $ense Ministry can be used by God to remove a major stumbling block to spiritual growth and development. When money is no longer the chief rival god, when money no longer controls the person but the person controls money, and when the deceitfulness of riches is exposed and can no longer choke out God's Word (Matthew 13:22), individuals are freed up to relate to God and to serve God in profoundly new and deeper ways.

The *Good $ense Implementation Guide* is a road map to implementing a Good $ense Ministry in your church. It begins with an overview of the foundations for a Good $ense Ministry, and then describes the four-phase implementation process.

If you have not yet viewed the video, *Casting a Vision for Good $ense*, I encourage you to do so before proceeding.

My prayer for you and your church is that the *Good $ense Implementation Guide* will help you to envision the power of a Good $ense Ministry and how it can impact your congregation, your leadership, the ministry of your church, and even your community. My hope is not only that you will carefully follow the steps as they are laid out, but also that you will feel freedom within the steps to customize the process for the unique challenges and opportunities of your church and ministry.

From the beginning of your implementation process, I hope you will see that building a Good $ense Ministry is more than just following a step-by-step process, though we have worked hard to provide that for you. Building your own Good $ense Ministry will also require that you deepen your understanding of Biblical Financial Principles, and that you grow in your dependence on the power of the Holy Spirit as you seek to help others resist the incredibly strong pull of the competing theology called materialism.

God bless you as you begin this important journey.

Dick Towner

FOUNDATIONS OF THE GOOD $ENSE MINISTRY MOVEMENT

The Good $ense Ministry movement is a ministry of the Willow Creek Association devoted to the cause of transformational stewardship for today's church.

Mission Statement

The mission of the Good $ense Ministry movement is to empower church leaders to implement biblically-based stewardship ministries within the local church. Our goal is that it become normative for the local church—your church—to regularly teach and train people in biblical stewardship. We desire to envision, equip, and encourage Christian leaders to build year-round, integrated, biblically-based stewardship ministries in the local church; and to assist in the growth process that moves every believer toward spiritual and financial freedom and responsibility.

Strategy

To accomplish this mission, the Good $ense Ministry movement has a twofold strategy: 1) to teach and train every believer in the Biblical Financial Principles of money management; and 2) to train and equip a few to provide biblical counsel. We act on this strategy by developing, disseminating, and supporting the use of culturally relevant, biblically-based, and easily understood stewardship resources within the local church. The two foundational Good $ense resources are the *Good $ense Budget Course* and the *Good $ense Counselor Training Workshop.*

We created the *Good $ense Budget Course* to proclaim God's truth and train every believer to integrate Biblical Financial Principles into their lives. This course addresses:

- What the culture says about money. We call this the "Pull of the Culture."

- What the Bible says about money. We call this the "Mind and Heart of God," and explore how it contrasts with the Pull of the Culture.

- The tools, insights, and information by which a person can implement the Biblical Financial Principles in their own life.

- The motivation and encouragement needed to do so!

We created the *Good $ense Counselor Training Workshop* to train and equip a team of budget counselors to provide free, biblically-based, confidential counsel to assist families and individuals in addressing financial difficulties or, better yet, to help them avoid encountering financial difficulties to begin with.

Whom We Serve

Those served by the Good $ense Ministry in the local church—Good $ense clients—typically find themselves in one of four financial situations:

- *In crisis.* These folks are experiencing serious financial problems, requiring immediate help and ongoing encouragement and assistance.

- *One paycheck from disaster.* These people aren't experiencing any immediate crisis, but they are living from paycheck-to-paycheck. They sense that their debt is too high and their savings too low. However, they are often lulled into a false sense of security by the cultural message that everything is okay as long as they are making minimum payments on their debts.

- *Good "financial" shape.* This group is not in consumer debt, they save on a regular basis, and they invest wisely. From a purely financial standpoint, they are good money managers. But they haven't yet grasped the vision of leading a financial lifestyle from a Christian perspective.

- *God-honoring lifestyle.* This group has applied the Biblical

Financial Principles to their lives. They understand that they have been entrusted with what belongs to God, and they are handling their finances in a God-honoring way. Good $ense Ministry leaders and counselors are drawn from this group.

Although the majority of Good $ense clients will be in the "in crisis" or "one paycheck from disaster" situations, *it is vital that the Good $ense Ministry be presented to your church as a ministry that serves people in every financial situation.* Because people in every economic situation need to be grounded in and living according to Biblical Financial Principles, Good $ense counselors are available not just for those in difficulty but also for those who want additional guidance on honoring God with their finances. For example, the person who receives an inheritance and wants advice on how to handle it wisely; the person who has been living within his or her means and has recently earned a significant pay raise; the engaged couple with two incomes who want to save wisely for their first home; the person of significant means who wants to understand more deeply what Scripture says about finances and how he or she can live that out.

The Importance of a Good $ense Ministry

For many people, money is a chief rival god. This fact puts the Good $ense Ministry movement and the local church ministry at the forefront of spiritual warfare. Money can be a spiritual ally or a spiritual enemy. As an ally, money enables us to do God's work in the world and provide comfort and joy for ourselves and others; as an enemy, it can create barriers that inhibit God's work and cause us to falter on the path to spiritual growth and transformation.

The Bible is clear that an improper relationship to money can:

- Keep us from serving God. We can only serve one master (Matthew 6:24).

- Steal our hearts from God. Where our treasure is our hearts will be (Matthew 6:21).

- Choke out the Word of God in our lives and make us unfruitful. Jesus said the weeds and the vines in the parable of the sower were the deceitfulness of riches (Matthew 13:22).

- Lead to all kinds of evil (1 Timothy 6:10).

These four verses alone, not to mention 2,300 others throughout Scripture that deal with the topic of money, should convince us of the vital importance of this issue for every church and every believer.

The Benefits of a Good $ense Ministry[1]

The most significant benefit of a Good $ense Ministry in the local church is that God can use it to remove money as a major stumbling block to spiritual growth and transformation.[2] Lives will be changed as individuals are freed from the crush of consumer debt and come to a deeper understanding of what it means to be a trustee—rather than an owner—of the resources God has entrusted to them. Marriages will be strengthened as money ceases to be a contentious issue in family life and decisions. Your church's ability to fulfill its vision and mission will increase as more and more believers are freed up to give with glad and generous hearts.

A Good $ense Ministry also provides a meaningful way to reach out beyond the walls of your church into the community. Just think of the impact you could have in the lives of unchurched people when you offer to help with their financial difficulties or challenges!

---

[1] Refer to pages 82–84 of the Appendix for more information on these benefits.
[2] The key to this is becoming aware of areas where the Pull of the Culture tempts us and understanding how Biblical Financial Principles can counteract those temptations (see Appendix pages 77–79).

THE IMPLEMENTATION PROCESS

The Road Map

The *Good $ense Implementation Guide* can be understood as a road map that will guide you to the ultimate destination—a thriving Good $ense Ministry in your church. The implementation process described in these pages shows the recommended route for launching and implementing your ministry. As with any map, there are certainly alternate routes you can take, and you may choose to adapt the route to your unique circumstances. However, it is important to note that to develop an effective Good $ense Ministry, you must travel through all four phases:

- Phase 1: Commitment
- Phase 2: Development
- Phase 3: Launch
- Phase 4: Expansion

These phases include laying a leadership foundation, training Good $ense counselors for year-round ministry, annually presenting the *Good $ense Budget Course* multiple times, and integrating the Good $ense Ministry into the life of other ministries throughout the church.

It is our hope and recommendation that you begin by establishing a complete and ongoing Good $ense Ministry. If it is not possible for you to do so at this time, you may opt to begin modestly and then work toward launching a fully integrated ministry. As a starting point, you may teach the *Good $ense Budget Course* but wait to create a core team and train counselors. If you choose this approach as a first step, portions of the process will still be helpful to you in presenting the *Good $ense Budget Course.* Should you decide to use the success of the *Good $ense Budget Course* to launch an ongoing ministry, you can do so by going back and working through all four phases of the implementation process.

The four phases of implementing a Good $ense Ministry each include several action steps:

Phase 1: Commitment
Step 1: Obtain preliminary support from senior church leadership
Step 2: Commission a Good $ense Ministry champion
Step 3: Form a Good $ense Ministry core team
Step 4: Educate the ministry champion and core team
Step 5: Develop a Good $ense vision statement for your church
Step 6: Prepare a Good $ense Ministry proposal
Step 7: Secure commitment from senior church leadership

Phase 2: Development
Step 1: Recruit volunteers for Good $ense Ministry positions
Step 2: Identify a Good $ense administrator and set up the Good $ense Ministry office
Step 3: Select and train Good $ense teachers
Step 4: Select and train Good $ense counselors
Step 5: Set up and initiate counseling (and teaching) teams

Phase 3: Launch
Step 1: Communicate the Good $ense Ministry vision to the congregation and promote the *Good $ense Budget Course*
Step 2: Teach the *Good $ense Budget Course*
Step 3: Offer counseling services
Step 4 Evaluate the *Good $ense Budget Course* and counseling services
Step 5: Celebrate successes
Step 6: Implement Good $ense Ministry improvements

Phase 4: Expansion
Step 1: Select and train additional counselors
Step 2: Increase the number and variety of Good $ense courses
Step 3: Seek opportunities to partner with other church ministries

The pages that follow provide an overview of all four phases, including the purpose, steps, and importance of each phase as well as detailed descriptions of each step within that phase. At the end of every overview is an action plan chart you can use to track progress. Before moving on to the next phase, there are also questions to help you discern whether or not that the phase is complete. For additional help, see pages 85–88 in the Appendix, which address common questions about implementing a Good $ense Ministry.

It's been said you never get a second chance to make a good first impression. The same could be said of launching a new ministry. To effectively launch a thriving Good $ense Ministry, it is vitally important to lay a firm foundation by beginning with steps in the first phase and then following the steps in every subsequent phase until all the steps have been completed. Doing so will help you to develop a broad base of support for the ministry within your congregation. It will also provide you with peace of mind, knowing you have taken all the necessary steps for launching a dynamic ministry God can use to profoundly change lives.

PHASE 1: COMMITMENT

PHASE 1: COMMITMENT

OVERVIEW

Purpose

The purpose of this phase is to secure commitment from a Good $ense Ministry champion, core team, and senior church leadership.

Steps

During this phase, preliminary support from senior church leadership is obtained, a ministry champion is commissioned, a Good $ense core team is formed and educated, a Good $ense vision and a proposal are prepared, and ongoing commitment is secured from senior church leadership.

Importance

In order for a Good $ense Ministry to reach its potential as a fully integrated ministry of your church, it is necessary to have a committed ministry champion and core team who feel called to provide sustained leadership, a vision to keep the ministry on course, and a detailed proposal so that senior leadership can fully commit to the requirements of the ministry. Without these components, a Good $ense Ministry may be able to conduct a few courses and counsel a few people, but it will fail to maximize the impact it could have in transforming hearts and lives.

STEPS 1-7

Step 1: Obtain preliminary support from senior church leadership

In order to initiate a Good $ense Ministry, one must secure preliminary support from senior church leadership. The best way to do this is to meet informally, one-on-one with senior leaders. Share what you know about the Good $ense Ministry—how you became aware of Good $ense, the Good $ense mission statement and strategies, the benefits of a Good $ense Ministry, and whom the ministry serves. If possible, show the *Casting a Vision for Good $ense* video. Speak and listen from the heart. Ask for their support in forming a core team that will create a vision and formal ministry proposal for your church.

Step 2: Commission a Good $ense Ministry champion

What is a ministry champion?

The ministry champion has a passion to help people develop God-honoring practices and perspectives on finances, so they might experience spiritual and financial freedom, and feels led to initiate a Good $ense Ministry. This is the person who leads the core team through the four implementation phases—Commitment, Development, Launch, and Expansion.

Why is a ministry champion necessary?

Implementing a Good $ense Ministry involves more than teaching a course. It is an ongoing, multifaceted ministry requiring substantial time, human resources, and financial commitment. In such a situation, a point person who can cast vision and rally people around the vision is key. It is critical that an individual considering the role of ministry champion be familiar with every aspect of this challenging task. Identifying and commissioning an appropriately gifted and impassioned ministry champion is a crucial step to launching an effective Good $ense Ministry.

What gifts and skills does the ministry champion need?

In addition to having a passion for biblical financial management, the primary spiritual gift required of the ministry champion is leadership—the ability to form, direct, and build team unity and to spiritually motivate others. A gifted leader has the skills to articulate the Good $ense vision to church leadership and the congregation. They should have the ability to overcome resistance and objections that often arise in any discussion of money in a church context.

A secondary gift required is that of administration—the ability to plan, arrange, prioritize, and implement.

There is a sample job description for the ministry champion in the Appendix on page 105.

While it may be difficult to find one person who embodies all the desired skills and spiritual gifts, the ministry champion should have the ability to recruit others whose strengths cover the areas he or she lacks.

How is the ministry champion identified and commissioned?

First, pray and seek the guidance of the Holy Spirit. The objective is not just to find a warm body to fill the slot, but to identify the right person, with the right gifts, who has a passion for biblical financial management and feels called by God to lead the ministry. In many cases it will be someone who has the reputation of being generous and of handling their finances wisely. The ministry champion may well be you, the individual who first picked up this Implementation Guide.

Once the ministry champion has been identified and has agreed to accept the leadership role, he or she is officially commissioned. Commissioning means being recognized in an "official" way in a public gathering, most likely a worship service, and being set apart for the ministry. The purpose of commissioning is to give the ministry champion the official blessing of senior leadership and to empower them to take the next steps in initiating a Good $ense Ministry.

Cautions

The ministry champion must clearly understand the commitment of time and personal energy required to successfully launch a Good $ense Ministry. Since the ministry is year-round and multifaceted, and since getting something new off the ground requires extra effort, it is reasonable to suggest that the leadership of a Good $ense Ministry will take one's full-time volunteer efforts.

If the ministry champion is a financial services professional, it must be recognized that they are not permitted to benefit financially in any way through their involvement in the ministry.

Step 3: Form a Good $ense Ministry core team

What is a core team?

A core team is a group of four to six individuals who assist the ministry champion in leading the Good $ense Ministry.

Why is a core team necessary?

The core team members bring a range of viewpoints, gifts, and skills to handling the many facets of initiating the ministry. The core team:

- assists the ministry champion in preparing and presenting the Good $ense Ministry vision and proposal
- oversees and participates in the implementation process
- provides ongoing leadership to the ministry once it is established

What gifts and skills do core team members need?

It is helpful to have a well-rounded group of core team members with a variety of gifts and skills. An ideal team might consist of individuals specializing in counseling, budgeting or finance, communications, adult education, and administration.

There is a sample position description for core team members in the Appendix on page 106.

How are core members recruited and selected?

Forming a Good $ense core team includes the following activities:

- **Inform the congregation.**
  With senior church leadership's approval, inform the congregation about the forthcoming formation of a Good $ense Ministry core team. Invite those who are interested to attend an informational meeting to learn more. In some churches, the ministry champion may be permitted to do this by "sounding a call" from the pulpit; that is, briefly explaining the ministry and asking any others who feel called to the ministry to identify themselves. Announcements in weekly bulletins, as well as in the church newsletter or on its web site, are also good vehicles for getting the word out. Use of the video *Casting a Vision for Good $ense* may be helpful. In addition, one-on-one recruiting by the ministry champion is appropriate, and often most effective.

- **Hold an informational meeting.**
  Once you've generated interest, hold an informational meeting so people can learn more and take the next step toward involvement. During the meeting, the ministry champion would:
  - Show the *Casting a Vision for Good $ense* video.
  - Describe the role of the core team and the types of skills needed.
  - Answer any questions attendees may have.
  - Observe the level of enthusiasm, obvious giftedness, and any initial sense of chemistry among attendees.
  - Ask attendees to fill out a Volunteer Application expressing interest in being a core team member or to indicate whether they would prefer to be contacted for other positions at a later date (see page 153 of the Appendix).

- **Engage in one-on-one discussions with potential core team members.**
  Consider the applications and select what appears to be a well-rounded core team, that is, a team that includes various gifts and experiences such as those mentioned under "What gifts and skills do core team members need?" on the previous page. Invite each member to come in for a one-on-one discussion. Ask them about:

- their faith journey
- their reasons for wanting to be a core team member
- their gifts and skills
- how they handle their finances
- their availability for meetings

Allow them to ask you any additional questions they have about the ministry. Use this opportunity to share your own vision and enthusiasm for the ministry.

- **Issue formal invitations to join the core team.**
  Prayerfully select four to six individuals and formally invite them to form the core team. There is a sample invitation in the Appendix on page 111.

- **Secure commitments from core team members.**
  Hold an initial meeting and ask core team members to sign the Core Team Commitment Form (see page 155 in the Appendix), committing to the following:

  - To faithfully attend core team member meetings including training courses or visits to other ministries
  - To diligently study with the other core team members to more fully understand the Biblical Financial Principles
  - To honor the Biblical Financial Principles in their personal lives
  - To work as a team member to develop the proposal for a Good $ense Ministry and to provide ongoing leadership to the ministry

Those who did not emerge as core team members should be informed and assured that they will be contacted regarding other opportunities once the ministry has been approved by senior church leadership.

Step 4: Educate the ministry champion and core team

An excellent experience for a newly formed core team is to visit a church with an existing Good $ense Ministry and participate in the *Good $ense Budget Course* and the *Good $ense Counselor Training Workshop.* You may also want to observe a core team meeting, a counseling team meeting, and/or meet with the other church's core team members and

PHASE 1: COMMITMENT

their ministry champion. To locate the church nearest you with a Good $ense Ministry, go to the Willow Creek Association Good $ense Ministry movement web site at www.GoodSenseMinistry.com.

In addition, the core team should study together to develop their understanding of Biblical Financial Principles. See page 123 in the Appendix for Recommended Resources.

Step 5: Develop a Good $ense vision statement for your church

What is a vision statement?

A vision statement describes the preferred future for the Good $ense Ministry at your church. It also contains a mission statement, the strategies of your ministry, the benefits to the people, leadership, and the church, and an overview of the ministry's plans.

Why is the vision statement important?

A well-crafted vision statement articulates the scope of the ministry so that everyone who chooses to participate in volunteer positions understands what they are committing to. It communicates the importance and potential impact of the ministry and enables the ministry champion and the core team to develop leadership support and volunteer commitment to the ministry.

How is the vision statement developed?

- Appoint one team member to be the recorder. The recorder documents the team's thoughts about the vision statement.
- As a team, review the *Casting a Vision for Good $ense* video, the mission statement and strategies for the Good $ense Ministry movement, and the sample Good $ense Ministry Proposal in the Appendix on page 99.
- Discuss what components of these resources are important to include in the vision for your church.
- Consider how the Holy Spirit may be shaping your vision in ways that are unique and exciting.
- Have the recorder write and distribute an initial draft of the ministry vision.

- Ask team members to review the draft and pray about it before attending the next meeting.
- Discuss and refine the draft as needed. Several drafts may be necessary before the team is satisfied that the document conveys the vision for the ministry as they see it.
- With the vision clarified, determine what steps need to be taken to bring the vision into reality. Much of this Implementation Guide is about helping you determine those steps. The vision and the subsequent action steps form the basis for your ministry proposal.

Step 6: Prepare a Good $ense Ministry proposal

What is a Good $ense Ministry proposal?

A Good $ense Ministry Proposal is the strategic plan for your ministry. It describes the vision of the church and the Good $ense Ministry and tells how the Good $ense vision supports the church vision. It contains a mission statement, ministry strategies, ministry benefits, and an overview of ministry plans. It articulates ministry resource requirements, provides publicity plans and course offerings, proposes implementation timelines, and addresses any concerns unique to your church.

Why is a Good $ense Ministry Proposal necessary?

A well-prepared proposal is a great aid in establishing credibility with and securing the support of senior church leadership.

How is a Good $ense Ministry Proposal developed?

The core team can follow the format of the sample Good $ense Ministry Proposal on page 99 or develop your own format.

Step 7: Secure commitment from senior church leadership

What type of leadership commitment is necessary?

Senior church leadership must commit to the Good $ense Ministry both personally and organizationally.

- *Personal Commitment.* As individuals, senior church leaders need to personally understand and believe in the Good $ense Ministry and be willing to model the values of the ministry as part of their lives. They should grasp the significance of the ministry as a key way to assist individuals—themselves included—in their spiritual growth as well as educating and training them in biblical management of their resources. They should have a sense of the ministry's potential financial and spiritual impact on both members individually and the church corporately.

- *Organizational Commitment.* Senior church leaders also need to commit to encouraging and assisting the implementation process (i.e., commit staff, budget, and facilities). They need to be willing to make organizational changes and adjustments as necessary.

Why is senior church leadership commitment important?

Senior church leadership support is important to successfully launch a new ministry. Leadership can give a new ministry more visibility with a few carefully chosen comments in a public forum than all the posters you can have printed. The reaction of many people to the ministry will be a reflection of the support they sense it has from senior church leadership. Support is particularly necessary for the Good $ense Ministry because the topic of money is such a highly sensitive one and the ministry may, in its early stages, receive some negative reaction from persons who mistakenly—and unbiblically!—think the church should not talk about money.

How is senior church leadership support obtained?

Senior church leadership support is formally obtained at the time the ministry proposal is presented to them. Steps leading up to the presentation of the proposal include:

- *Meet one-on-one again with senior church leaders.* Share the "draft" of the ministry proposal. Listen, seek to understand, and identify any concerns with the proposal so that they can be properly addressed.

- *Refine the proposal.* The refined proposal should address any of the concerns that emerged in the one-on-one meetings. If you do this step well, the final acceptance of the proposal should be something of a formality.

- *Prepare the presentation of the proposal.* Keep in mind that the presentation should be concise—fifteen minutes or less plus time for questions—yet thorough. A recommended outline is:
  - Introduce core team members.
  - Briefly summarize the progress of the team to date (church visits, courses attended, group study, preparation of vision, preparation of proposal).
  - Present the proposal; summarize its key points.
  - Respond to questions.
  - Ask for leaders' personal and organizational commitment to the ministry including:
    - Regular teaching throughout the year from the pulpit about what God's Word says about our relationship to our money. Note that this goes far deeper than traditional teaching about giving associated with the annual "stewardship campaign." A list of audio taped messages given on this topic at Willow Creek appears on page 125 in the Appendix. You may wish to share these resources with your pastor(s).
    - Preaching/teaching by the pastor(s) expressing verbal support for the ministry to the congregation as the ministry organizes and prepares to offer its first budget courses.
    - Willingness to support and personally participate in the *Good $ense Budget Course* (to internalize the values of the ministry, be impacted personally by the course, and set an example for the congregation).
    - Approval to go ahead with the ministry implementation and assurance of the necessary funding, office space, etc.

As the presentation is being prepared:

- Determine the roles of core team members in the presentation.
- Set a time and place to present the proposal and confirm who will attend.
- Rehearse.
- Prepare copies of the proposal to use as handouts.
- Pray.

Caution

If your senior church leadership is not yet willing to support a Good $ense Ministry, *stop here.* Take the time to find out what their objections are and what issues still need to be addressed. Be sensitive but firm in asking how to justify *not* teaching and training people in a holistic manner in light of the following realities:

- the strong and counter-scriptural messages of the culture
- the havoc wreaked in lives and marriages by poor money management
- the power of money to keep us from serving God (Matthew 6:24); steal our hearts from God (Matthew 6:21); and choke out the Word of God in our lives (Matthew 13:22).

A person's relationship to their money and stuff is so intimately tied to their spiritual growth and development that it is vitally important to place a high priority on helping them get it right.

ACTION PLAN FOR PHASE 1: COMMITMENT

Step	Description	Responsibility	Target Date for Completion	Actual Completion Date
1	Obtain preliminary support from senior church leadership	Initiator of ministry		
2	Commission a Good $ense Ministry champion	Senior church leadership		
3	Form a Good $ense Ministry core team	Ministry champion		
	• Inform the congregation			
	• Hold an informational meeting			
	• Engage in one-on-one discussions with potential core team members			
	• Issue formal invitations to join the core team			
	• Secure commitments from core team members			
4	Educate the ministry champion and core team	Ministry champion, core team		
5	Develop a Good $ense vision statement for your church	Ministry champion, core team		
6	Prepare a Good $ense Ministry proposal	Ministry champion, core team		
7	Secure commitment from senior church leadership	Ministry champion, core team		

PHASE 1: COMMITMENT

❏ Has the ministry champion been commissioned?

❏ Is the core team committed and educated?

❏ Have the Good $ense vision and proposal been presented?

❏ Is your senior church leadership personally and organizationally committed?

Go no farther in the process until you have senior church leadership support. If you skip this phase and do not receive senior church leadership support, a Good $ense Ministry will not ultimately develop on a church-wide basis.

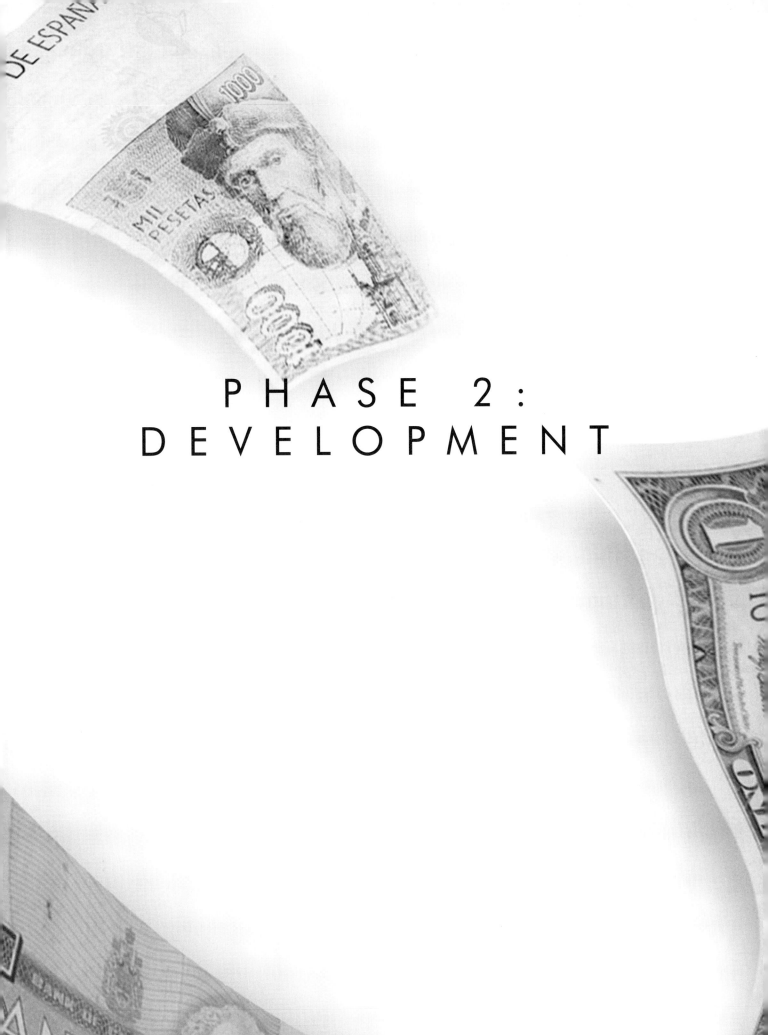

PHASE 2: DEVELOPMENT

PHASE 2: DEVELOPMENT

OVERVIEW

Purpose

The purpose of the development phase is to prepare counselors, teachers, and any support people so that they are in place when the Good $ense Ministry goes "public."

Steps

In this phase, volunteers will be recruited and trained, the ministry office will be set up, and counseling groups will begin meeting.

Importance

The teachers and counselors will be on the front lines of implementing the ministry vision. It is critical that these individuals are thoroughly trained in their roles and that they have the support they need.

Caution

The Good $ense Ministry will not be successful without volunteers who have the appropriate spiritual gifts. *Network,* a curriculum and ministry that helps individuals discover and employ their spiritual gifts, is an excellent tool for this purpose. For more information on *Network,* visit the Willow Creek Association website: www.willowcreek.com.

STEPS 1-5

Step 1: Recruit volunteers for the Good $ense Ministry team

Initially, the most important roles to fill are those of the Good $ense administrator, teachers, and counselors. The Good $ense administrator is needed to set up the Good $ense Ministry office and procedures so the infrastructure is in place for training and counseling. Teachers are needed to conduct the *Good $ense Counselor Training Workshop* and *Good $ense Budget Course.* Counselors need to be ready to help during the *Good $ense Budget Course* and to provide follow-up after the course. As the ministry grows, it may be necessary to add additional positions such as an events coordinator or communications positions.

Why is recruiting important?

As the ministry begins and the number of people it serves grows, the need for dedicated ministry volunteers grows as well. While some roles may be carried out by members of the core team in the early stages of the ministry, core team members will increasingly need to devote their time to overall direction and vision for the ministry.

How is recruiting accomplished?

- *Prepare ministry position descriptions.* Sample position descriptions are in the Appendix on pages 105–110.

- *Publicize the needs and recruit throughout the church.* Personal one-on-one recruiting by members of the core team is often very effective. Stress the significance and rewards of being involved in such a life-changing ministry as Good $ense. Obviously, the people who initially expressed interest in the ministry but did not become core team members are prime candidates.

Step 2: Select a Good $ense administrator and set up the Good $ense Ministry office

What is a Good $ense administrator?

The Good $ense administrator coordinates the administrative functions of the ministry. He or she is responsible for the forms, the files, and the counseling procedures. The administrator pairs counselors with clients and assists with registration for teaching and training events. There is a position description for this position in the Appendix on page 107.

What needs to be accomplished to set up the Good $ense Ministry office?

- *Secure the space necessary for files and materials.* Remember, much of the information the ministry will handle is very confidential and ensuring it will stay that way is central to the ministry's credibility.

- *Set up a phone line with voice mail.* Multiple mailboxes can help handle inquiries by clients and volunteers.

- *Make copies of all necessary counseling forms.* Hard copies of these forms are provided for you in the Appendix. Electronic copies are included on the *Good $ense Counselor Training Workshop* PowerPoint CD-ROM.

- *Determine the procedures you will use for counseling.* This includes how clients enter the ministry, how they are matched with counselors, and how client progress is tracked. There is a sample procedure in the Appendix on page 103.

Step 3: Select and train Good $ense teachers

Why are Good $ense teachers important?

A core strategy of the Good $ense Ministry is course offerings which present Biblical Financial Principles, contrast them with the messages of our culture, and present practical ways to live them out. Teachers are the ones who will facilitate this learning.

How are Good $ense teachers selected?

First and foremost among criteria for selecting teachers are a passion for this ministry and spiritual maturity. Ideally, the person would have the gift of teaching; however, every effort has been made to give the teachers of the *Good $ense Counselor Training Workshop* and the *Good $ense Budget Course* all the material and supplemental help they need to make a world class presentation. We also strongly recommend that you find people with the motivation to take the time to "own the material"—to add their own examples, to be certain they are familiar with the PowerPoint or overhead and video components, etc. Candidates for these positions may have teaching strengths but be weak on their understanding of Biblical Financial Principles; their commitment must also include a willingness to study and grow in this area. There is a sample position description for this position in the Appendix on page 108.

The Volunteer Application form in the Appendix on page 153 may also be used for this position. A personal interview should follow the application process. A sample interview outline appears on page 114 of the Appendix along with a list of qualifications of a Good $ense teacher on page 112.

Although one teacher could teach both courses, it is recommended that you begin with at least two teachers to teach the *Good $ense Budget Course* and *Good $ense Counselor Training Workshop*.

Once a person has been selected, preparation to teach includes the following:

- Have them thoroughly read the Leader's Guide.

- Hold practice sessions with other teachers or core team members asking participants to evaluate them. Videotape these sessions if possible and perform a self-evaluation.

- Have them read recommended resources (see page 123) to deepen their understanding of Biblical Financial Principles.

- If possible, it would be helpful to visit another church to experience the *Good $ense Budget Course* or *Good $ense Counselor Training Workshop* as a participant.

- For those teaching the *Good $ense Budget Course,* consider holding a pilot course. Invite senior church leaders, core team members, and counselors. A pilot course provides a valuable training experience for the teacher(s) and also enables leaders to see the course before it is rolled out to the congregation.

Step 4: Select and train Good $ense counselors

Why are Good $ense counselors important?

Counselors are a key component of the overall Good $ense Ministry strategy. Three things are necessary for many people to successfully handle their material resources in a way that leads to spiritual growth and financial freedom and responsibility. First, they must be taught what the Biblical Financial Principles are concerning the use of money. Teaching answers the question, *"What* does the Bible say?" Second, they must be trained in how to apply those principles to their daily lives. Training answers the question, *"How* do I apply the Biblical principles to my life?" Third, they must be held accountable and encouraged. Although counselors uniquely do teach and train, they also provide that third, often vital, ingredient—a mix of accountability and reinforcement of what has been taught. They provide encouragement and hope in the face of the "pull of the culture" which so seductively counters the Biblical Financial Principles and undermines resolve to change.

In addition, the impact of the *Good $ense Budget Course* and other Good $ense courses will be significantly enhanced if a cadre of trained counselors is on hand to assist participants during the course and to provide follow-up to those requesting it.

How are Good $ense counselors selected?

Counselor selection should be done very carefully. Counselors are entrusted with an individual or family in a very sensitive and spiritually significant area of their life. Counselors should be members of the church, mature in their faith journey, and living in accordance with the Biblical Financial Principles upon which the Good $ense Ministry is founded. It is not a volunteer responsibility to be entered into lightly or to be given to a spiritually immature person. A sample position description for the Good $ense counselor is in the Appendix on page 109.

The recommended selection procedure for counselors includes:

- *Application.* Prospective counselors are given a sheet outlining the qualifications and responsibilities of the position (see page 113 of the Appendix along with the Volunteer Application form on page 153). They are asked to complete the application and return it to the Good $ense office.

- *Interview.* The Good $ense Ministry champion or a member of the core team conducts an in-depth interview with the candidate. Topics explored include the person's faith journey, why they feel called to the ministry and how they are handling their finances in accord with Biblical Financial Principles. In addition, it is made very clear to those in financial service professions that they may not in any way benefit financially from their involvement in the ministry. This stipulation eliminates the possibility of a client purchasing product or paying for services from their counselor and protects the ministry from criticism in this area. A suggested outline for the counselor interview is in the Appendix on page 116.

How are counselors trained?

Following a successful interview, the candidate is asked to attend the *Good $ense Counselor Training Workshop,* is given the *Good $ense Counselor Training Workshop* Participant's Guide and Manual, and is asked to do the required pre-reading.

The *Good $ense Counselor Training Workshop* is an eight-hour course that covers the Biblical Financial Principles, the counseling process, and listening skills. Counselors are given the opportunity to practice counseling meetings before encountering an actual client. The Leader's Guide contains the information needed to conduct the *Good $ense Counselor Training Workshop.*

In addition, the initial group of counselors are also encouraged to attend the pilot *Good $ense Budget Course* so they can experience the course from a participant's viewpoint and can be better equipped to help during the church-wide offering of this course.

Periodic continuing education classes for all counselors sharpen their skills and provide good team-building opportunities. The Good $ense web site contains ideas for continuing counselor education.

Hint: Invite the core team to go through the *Good $ense Counselor Training Workshop* if they have not yet attended it at another church.

Step 5: Develop counseling (and teaching) groups

What are counseling groups?

A counseling group is at least three counselors who meet on a regular basis (at least once per month).

Why are counseling groups important?

Counseling groups can serve as a place where counselors can continue to practice their skills in a safe and non-threatening environment before meeting an actual client. Groups may also engage in study to deepen their understanding of the Biblical Financial Principles. (See Recommended Resources on page 123 in the Appendix. Some suggestions for the ways groups can be formed appear on pages 92–96.)

Once counseling begins, it is important that the counselors continue to meet regularly for skill development, community building, prayer, and group unity. Counseling is an individual, often demanding, and sometimes frustrating ministry role. Clients often find it difficult to change the habits of a lifetime, waiver in the discipline required to follow through on assignments, and sometimes miss scheduled appointments—all of which can be very discouraging to the counselor. Successful cases* can be expected to be fewer than half. Group meetings become a place to share victories, receive consolation for the losses, and be reminded that God is sovereign and that sometimes our role is to plant seeds that may not sprout until a later time.

How do teachers fit into these groups?

If your church has at least three teachers, it is suggested that they form their own teaching group. They can work together to practice the course material, and they can also engage in study to deepen their understanding of the Biblical Financial Principles.

---

* A successful case is defined as one in which the client has established a balanced budget and has maintained it for three months; a Debt Reduction Plan has been established and has been operative for three months; the client is making decisions based upon the Biblical Financial Principles; and the client is meeting the goals expressed in the application or during one of the first meetings with the counselor.

In many cases, a church may have only one or two teachers. If that is the case, each teacher should participate in one of the counseling groups. This will enhance their teaching by giving them examples of client and counselor challenges and success stories. In addition, it gives them a group with which to engage in deeper study. Since these teachers should have strong facilitation skills, they may even wish to take on the group leader responsibility described below.

How are group leaders selected?

Counselors and teachers who believe they have the gifts and desire to serve as a group leader are invited to make that known. Ask a prospective counselor to indicate their interest on the Volunteer Application form (page 153 of the Appendix); new or experienced counselors wishing to move into this role can verbally let the Good $ense Ministry champion know. A good time to recruit for group leaders is at the end of the *Good $ense Counselor Training Workshop.*

Selection is then done through an informal meeting between the candidate and the Good $ense Ministry champion or core team members.

What are the responsibilities of the group leader?

The group leader is charged with the responsibility of facilitating the meetings and building community within the group. The role is considered to be a key one within the ministry. Serving as a group leader does not require prior service within Good $ense. There is a position description on page 110 of the Appendix.

ACTION PLAN FOR PHASE 2: DEVELOPMENT

Step	Description	Responsibility	Target Date for Completion	Actual Completion Date
1	Recruit volunteers for the Good $ense Ministry team			
	• Prepare ministry position descriptions	Ministry champion, core team		
	• Publicize the needs and recruit throughout the church	Ministry champion, core team		
2	Select a Good $ense administrator and set up the Good $ense Ministry office	Ministry champion, core team		
	• Secure the office space necessary for files and materials	Ministry champion, administrator		
	• Set up a phone line with voice mail	Ministry champion, administrator		
	• Make copies of all necessary counseling forms	Administrator		
	• Determine the procedures you will use for counseling	Ministry champion, administrator		
3	Select and train Good $ense teachers	Ministry champion, core team		
	• Have them thoroughly read the Leader's Guide	Teachers		
	• Hold practice sessions with other teachers or core team members	Teachers		
	• Have them read recommended resources to deepen understanding of Biblical Financial Principles	Teachers		
	• Visit another church to experience course(s)	Teachers		
	• Hold a pilot *Good $ense Budget Course* for senior church leadership, core team members, and counselors	Ministry champion, core team, and teachers		

Step	Description	Responsibility	Target Date for Completion	Actual Completion Date
4	Select and train Good $ense counselors			
	• Accept applications of prospective counselors	Administrator		
	• Conduct in-depth interviews and select counselors	Ministry champion, core team		
	• Conduct the *Good $ense Counselor Training Workshop*	Ministry champion, core team, teacher		
5	Develop counseling (and teaching) teams	Ministry champion, core team		

❏ Is the Good $ense administrator in place and the Good $ense office set up?

❏ Is at least one teacher identified and trained for the *Good $ense Counselor Training Workshop* and the *Good $ense Budget Course?*

❏ Are counselors selected and trained?

❏ Are counseling teams with team leaders in place?

Complete each item before proceeding with the implementation process.

REVIEW OF PROGRESS

You're almost there!

Let's review what you've done so far. You have:

- gathered support from senior church leadership
- recruited a core team
- prepared a vision and proposal
- trained Good $ense teachers and counselors

Congratulations! That's a lot of work!

PHASE 3: LAUNCH

PHASE 3: LAUNCH

OVERVIEW

Purpose

The purpose of the launch phase is to go public with the first offerings of the ministry. It is the fulfillment of the tremendous efforts of your Good $ense core team to date.

Steps

In this phase, the vision will be communicated to the congregation, the *Good $ense Budget Course* will be presented, counseling services will begin, and the course and services will be evaluated with progress affirmed and action plans for improvement implemented.

Importance

There is only one chance to make a good impression as you prepare to go public with the Good $ense Ministry and offer the first *Good $ense Budget Course* and counseling services.

STEPS 1-6

Step 1: Communicate the Good $ense Ministry vision to the congregation and promote the *Good $ense Budget Course*

Ideally, the congregation has become partially aware of this new Good $ense Ministry as a result of the recruitment efforts that have already taken place. Now it is time to clearly communicate the Good $ense Ministry vision to the congregation and begin to promote the *Good $ense Budget Course.*

When should this be done?

An ideal time to begin this communication is in early January, with the *Good $ense Budget Course* being offered in late January or early February. The full impact of Christmas spending has hit and the concept of a New Year's resolution still has some validity. Another opportune time is early fall, as vacation bills and school expenses have created heightened awareness of family finances. A third good opportunity is mid- to late April, just after tax time. Ideally the course would be presented on an on-going basis at least twice per year.

How is this accomplished?

A significant aid to establishing the ministry and its vision, and to the success of the initial *Good $ense Budget Course,* is a well-timed series of teaching messages that have to do with what the Bible says about money and our relationship to it. This will demonstrate that the vision has been shared with and embraced by the pastoral staff. These messages should not focus on giving and should not be traditional stewardship messages simply presented at a different time of the year. It is very important that the Good $ense Ministry not be interpreted as simply a means of getting people to give more to the church. Needless to say, this would be disastrous to the ministry and undercut its basic purpose. Message tapes on finances that have been developed at Willow Creek are listed in the Appendix on page 125 and may be helpful. In addition, message transcripts, drama scripts, and some drama videos are available. See pages 125–127 in the Appendix. They can be ordered through the Willow Creek Association website at www.willowcreek.com.

Coordinated with the preaching message(s) should be a concentrated effort to communicate that the *Good $ense Budget Course* will be offered and that it is a foundational course, not just for those in financial difficulty, but for everyone who wishes to understand more deeply and apply more effectively what the Bible says about money management. You may safely say—and our experience is—that everyone, from the person who has never budgeted to the astute financial planner, will have much to learn.

Use several vehicles to promote the course. These could include announcements in weekly bulletins, the church newsletter, and church web site. You may also wish to create a brochure describing the course. An example of a brochure is included in the Appendix on pages 119–120.

Don't hesitate to be creative when promoting the course. In addition to printed materials, consider the use of drama in a worship service. The topic of budgeting often lends itself to humor. If used appropriately, humor can be very effective in lowering defenses and helping people to feel more at ease. Personal testimonies are also very effective. After holding your first course, there will be people whose lives and hearts are changed. Ask them if they would be willing to share their stories with the congregation prior to the next course offering.

Good $ense counseling services also need to be publicized. Inform the congregation that trained, confidential counselors are available to offer free, biblically-based, in-depth assistance to individuals and families.

Step 2: Teach the Good $ense Budget Course

Why is this important?

The *Good $ense Budget Course* is basic to everything the ministry teaches. Its applicability cuts across all economic levels and situations. It lays the foundational springboard for the other ministry offerings and provides a logical entry point for people to receive ongoing counseling. It provides a highly visible, church-wide event to draw attention to the launch of the ministry. In addition, it can serve as an excellent side door opportunity to invite those outside the church to an event that is highly relevant to their lives.

How is this accomplished?

The preferred way to publicly kick off the ministry is by offering the *Good $ense Budget Course* in a one-day workshop format to the whole church.

Ample time must be given for attendees to register ahead of time and do the pre-work which is necessary to realize maximum benefit from the course. *Registration should begin no less than three weeks before the date of the course.*

Before initiating registration, you will need to determine whether or not to charge a fee for the Participant's Guide. We have found that people are more committed to attending when they pay something up front.

Make the registration location convenient and the registration process simple and speedy. It works well to have registration tables set up outside of services. If your church has a web site, you may also want to offer electronic registration.

Pre-work is included in the *Good $ense Budget Course* Participant's Guide. An alternative to handing out the entire Participant's Guide at registration is to make copies of the pre-work and hand it out at registration. The Participant's Guide would then be distributed on the day of the course. A copy of the pre-work is included in the Appendix on pages 157–172 and on the *Good $ense Budget Course* PowerPoint CD-ROM. Pre-work could be e-mailed to those who register via web site. You may wish to personalize the cover of the pre-work packet and the cover letter to include information about time and place, lunch arrangements, etc.

Be sure all logistical information is clearly presented. This includes:
- starting time
- length of the course
- location
- lunch arrangements
- cost, etc.

An example of a registration confirmation letter that can be handed out with the Participant's Guide or pre-work is included in the Appendix on page 121.

When participants arrive at the course, the Participant's Guide or pre-work can serve as their admission ticket. Ideally, the ministry should have a record of course attendees. This can be useful for a variety of future purposes—follow-up, feedback, invitations to future course offerings, etc. Gathering addresses and phone numbers at the time the person registers to take the course can, however, make registration too time consuming. It is best to gather attendee information by circulating sign-up sheets the day of the course.

On the day of the course, counselors should be available to help the attendees as they develop their Spending Plan worksheet and work on other activities throughout the day. This is always a fruitful and exciting day for the counselors as they have multiple opportunities to assist attendees. They should be identified by name tags or other means and introduced at the start of the course along with a brief explanation of their role. They should also sit among the audience and personally introduce themselves as participants arrive.

All other information you will need to prepare for the *Good $ense Budget Course* is included in the *Good $ense Budget Course* Leader's Guide. There is also a *Good $ense Budget Course* Checklist in the Appendix on page 122.

Caution

When launching the ministry, it is ideal to present the pilot *Good $ense Budget Course* (for core team and teacher training purposes), *Good $ense Counselor Training Workshop,* and the church-wide *Good $ense Budget Course* within a sixty- to ninety-day timeframe. If more time is allowed between these courses, you may lose some momentum and energy.

Step 3: Offer counseling services

The conclusion of the *Good $ense Budget Course* is an ideal time to offer ongoing counseling services. Provide the phone number of the

Good $ense office and invite those who find they need additional help to call.

Caution

Be careful of over-promoting counseling services. Although your desire is to assist all those that need help, recognize that you are constrained by the number of counselors you have available. You may get inundated with calls if you make counseling sound mandatory for everyone.

Step 4: Evaluate the *Good $ense Budget Course* and counseling services

Good $ense Budget Course

At the conclusion of the course, participants are asked to complete an evaluation form from the back of their Participant's Guide. One way to evaluate the *Good $ense Budget Course* is by reviewing and summarizing these evaluations.

Also assess the opinions and ideas of the teachers, the counselors, and the core team. Gather testimonials from participants for whom the course is having a life-changing impact to be used in future publicity.

Counseling Services

One way to evaluate your counseling services is to have clients complete an evaluation form when their counseling concludes (see page 151 in the Appendix). Another way is to look at the percentage of successful cases. A successful case is defined as one in which the clients have established a balanced budget and have maintained it for three months, a Debt Reduction Plan has been operative for three months, the clients are making decisions based upon the Biblical Financial Principles, and the clients are in the process of meeting their goals.

It will take some time to get a handle on this measurement since the typical case takes four to six months. When these statistics do begin to be compiled, recognize that it is not uncommon for more than a majority of cases to not meet the criteria for success as we have defined it. When a case is not successful, counselors should not feel that they have been a failure. They have simply confronted a very difficult situation that does not always result in immediate success. Should a counseling case not be successful, we encourage counselors to continue to pray for the client. There have been many instances in which an unsuccessful case returns to the ministry for another try at counseling a year or more later and at that point has the additional motivation and life changes to become a successful case.

It is also important to talk with the counselors and find out where they need additional help with assisting their clients. They can tell you a lot more than the numbers will. Continuing education classes for counselors can then address those needs.

Step 5: Celebrate successes

Look at how far your ministry has come. Take the time to pause, to pray, and to thank God for the blessings he has provided to your ministry. Be encouraged to accept God's pleasure with what you are doing and the impact you are having in people's lives.

Recognize and thank senior church leadership, core team members, teachers, counselors, etc. for the importance of what they've done. Consider holding some type of "thank you" celebration for all who have been involved in the ministry launch.

Step 6: Implement Good $ense Ministry improvements

Develop action plans to respond to areas that need improvement. These items may include additional training for counselors or teachers, other avenues of publicity for the workshop or counseling services, additional ministry positions, etc.

ACTION PLAN FOR PHASE 3: LAUNCH

Step	Description	Responsibility	Target Date for Completion	Actual Completion Date
1	Communicate the Good $ense Ministry vision to the congregation and promote the *Good $ense Budget Course*	Ministry champion, core team, senior church leadership		
2	Teach the *Good $ense Budget Course*	Ministry champion, core team, teacher, counselors		
3	Offer counseling services	Ministry champion, core team, administrator, counselors		
4	Evaluate the *Good $ense Budget Course* and counseling services	Ministry champion, core team		
5	Celebrate successes	Ministry champion, core team		
6	Implement Good $ense Ministry improvements	Ministry champion, core team		

- ❏ Was the Good $ense vision communicated to the congregation?

- ❏ Was the *Good $ense Budget Course* taught to those interested in the congregation?

- ❏ Are counseling services available?

- ❏ Have you evaluated the *Good $ense Budget Course* and counseling services?

- ❏ Have you celebrated ministry successes and implemented ministry improvements?

If so, congratulations! Your ministry has been launched! Proceed to the next phase.

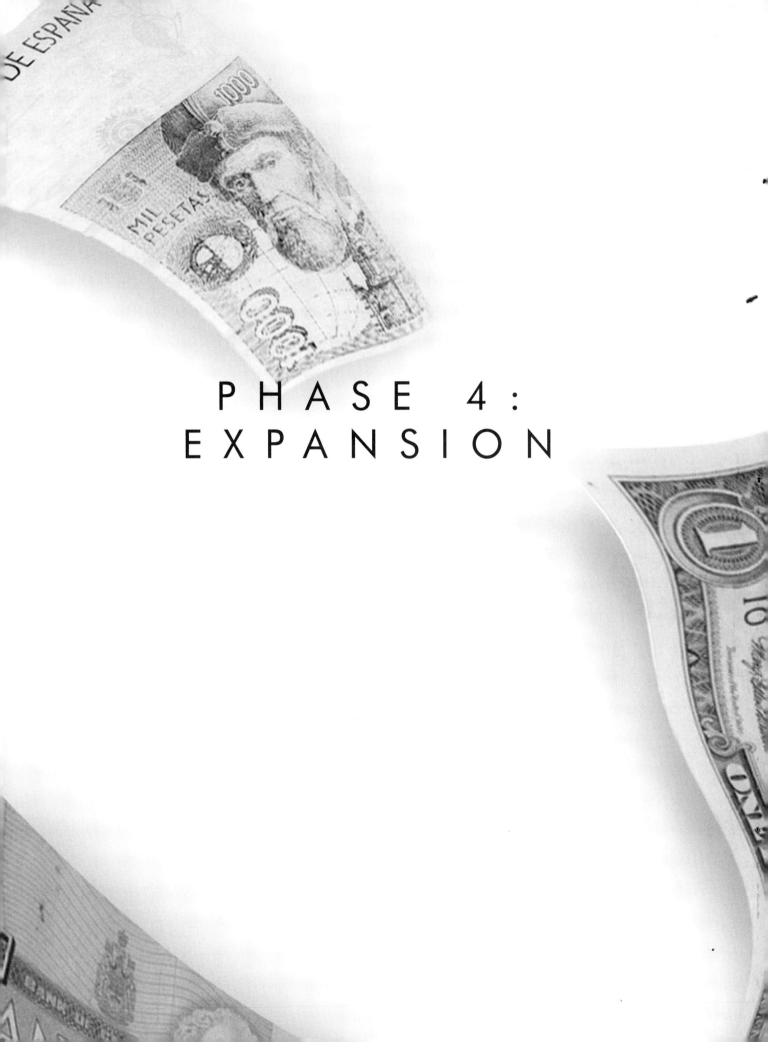

PHASE 4: EXPANSION

PHASE 4: EXPANSION

OVERVIEW

Purpose

The purpose of this phase is to develop the Good $ense Ministry into an ongoing, year-round integrated ministry. In this phase, we seek to expand both the counseling and teaching arms of the ministry and to establish ministry partnerships throughout the church in which Good $ense teaching can be customized to facilitate the goals of the other ministries while furthering the church-wide understanding of the Biblical Financial Principles on which Good $ense is based.

Steps

In this ongoing phase, additional counselors will be selected, the number and variety of Good $ense courses will be increased, and you will identify other church ministries to partner with.

Importance

Money and our relationship to it is a huge part of life and a huge part of our spiritual well-being and growth. Consequently, the Good $ense Ministry leadership should consistently look for appropriate ways in which the ministry can more fully serve the church at large. Specially adapted teaching and training opportunities for specific segments of the congregation can be an effective way to do so.

STEPS 1-3

Step 1: Select and train additional counselors

Why is this important?

Because many people have mismanaged their resources for so long, even when effective teaching takes place, one-on-one encouragement and accountability is often needed for them to be able to follow though. Once the Good $ense Ministry becomes public and word spreads concerning the availability of counseling, more counselors will be needed to meet the demand.

Another area for expansion of your counseling services is small group counseling. Some churches have begun offering counseling to small groups of people and it has proven to be very effective. See page 97 in the Appendix for tips on how to do this.

How?

Potential counselors should go through the selection and training process described on pages 42–43.

As you develop a cadre of experienced counselors, we suggest that new counselors be assigned a "mentor" and sit in on a session or two with them before receiving their first case. Likewise, the experienced counselor may observe the new counselor's first few counseling sessions to provide support and feedback.

Step 2: Increase the number and variety of Good $ense courses

Why is this important?

The *Good $ense Budget Course* has produced life-changing results in literally thousands of lives over the years. In many cases, individuals find it helpful to come to the course on repeated occasions for a review of concepts, new insights, and fresh encouragement. As word spreads concerning the impact of the course, additional people will wish to attend. In addition, there are a variety of other, more specific topics on which seminars and workshops can be held (see Step 3 below).

How?

Dates for the next *Good $ense Budget Course* should probably be set up even before the first course is held. Improvements for it and final planning details would flow out of the evaluations of the first workshop. While the full-day workshop is the recommended format, it should be noted that it can be presented in a number of different formats including six, fifty-minute sessions during, for example, adult Sunday school. As previously mentioned, a reasonable expectation is that the *Good $ense Budget Course* would be presented at least twice a year.

In addition, the Good $ense Ministry movement will be creating a series of additional, shorter courses on a wide variety of financial topics. Be sure to check the Good $ense website for information: www.GoodSenseMinistry.com.

Step 3: Seek opportunities to partner with other church ministries

Why is this important?

Our relationship to our money is not confined to one part of our lives but, in fact, impacts most—if not all—parts. Thus, the core teachings of the Good $ense Ministry have relevance to many ministries throughout the church.

How?

Be alert for how Good $ense can be helpful to and become a part of the core teaching in ministries throughout the church. Consider the following possibilities:

- Money issues lie at the heart of a large percentage of marital conflict. How can Good $ense teaching be a support to the marriage and pre-marriage ministry?
- Becoming a member of the church should carry with it a commitment to financial support of the church ministries. How can Good $ense be a part of the new member teaching process?

- Our young people are, in general, very misinformed about money. How can Good $ense equip parents to teach their children about a biblical view of money?
- How can Good $ense assist the benevolence ministry to make good decisions regarding helping folks who ask for financial assistance?
- Is there a trustworthy place a young couple can go for biblically-based counsel on how to deal with a significant inheritance? Where a couple nearing retirement can seek unbiased advice about financial questions?

The possibilities of how Good $ense can relate to and impact other ministries are only limited by one's imagination.

Watch the Good $ense Ministry website, www.GoodSenseMinistry.com, for ideas and for new course offerings that can be helpful in this partnering effort.

ACTION PLAN FOR PHASE 4: EXPANSION

Step	Description	Responsibility	Target Date for Completion	Actual Completion Date
1	Select and train additional counselors	Ministry champion, core team, teachers		
2	Increase the number and variety of Good $ense courses (write in course names below)	Ministry champion, core team		
3	Seek opportunities to partner with other church ministries (write in names of possible ministries below)	Ministry champion, core team		

❏ Are additional counselors trained?

❏ Have you increased the number and variety of Good $ense courses?

❏ Have you partnered with other ministries?

Dear Good $ense Ministry Champion:

Congratulations! You have everything in place for a fully integrated Good $ense Ministry! Only God knows how the ministry will be used in the days and years ahead. Can you imagine . . .

- How many lives will be spiritually deepened because their relationship to money now follows biblical guidelines?
- How many marriages will be restored and strengthened because conflict over money has been eliminated?
- How much anxiety and stress will be relieved as consumer debt is eliminated?
- How many young people will start out life implementing biblical wisdom into their monetary decisions?
- How many additional resources will be made available to God's work in the world?
- How many persons will be brought to Christ because the church reached out to them in an incredibly relevant area of their lives?

Only God knows for certain, but you can dream. And do so! Allow the vision of what could be to sustain, motivate, and energize you in your Good $ense leadership role.

In God's name and power,

Dick Towner
Good $ense Ministry Movement
Willow Creek Association

APPENDIX

APPENDIX CONTENTS

GOOD $ENSE MINISTRY

The Pull of the Culture vs. the Mind and Heart of God 74
The Biblical Financial Principles: Foundation of the Good
    $ense Ministry 77
Biblical Financial Principles 80
Benefits of a Good $ense Ministry .82
Questions and Answers about Implementing a Good $ense Ministry . .85
Removing Common Barriers that Make It Difficult to Speak about
    Money from the Pulpit 89
Small Groups within Good $ense .92
Tips for Group Counseling 97
Good $ense Ministry Proposal 99
Counseling Procedure 103

PERSONNEL / POSITIONS

Sample Position Description for Ministry Champion 105
Sample Position Description for Core Team Members 106
Sample Position Description for Administrator 107
Sample Position Description for Teacher 108
Sample Position Description for Counselor 109
Sample Position Description for Group Leader 110
Sample Invitation to Core Team Members 111
Qualifications of a Good $ense Teacher 112
Qualifications of a Good $ense Counselor 113
Interview Outline for Teachers 114
Interview Outline for Counselors .116

GOOD $ENSE BUDGET COURSE*

Sample *Good $ense Budget Course* Publicity 119
Sample *Good $ense Budget Course* Registration
    Confirmation Letter 121
Good $ense Budget Course Checklist 122

* The *Good $ense Budget Course* pre-work is included in the "Forms" section on page 157–172.

RECOMMENDED RESOURCES 123

FORMS

Client Profile 129
Tips for Filling Out Your Client Profile 133
Client Profile Analysis Chart 135
Good $ense Budget Counseling Covenant 139
Spending Record 141
Spending Plan 143
Debt Reduction Plan 145
Client Progress Report 147
Case Completion Report 149
Client Counseling Evaluation Form 151
Volunteer Application 153
Core Team Commitment Form 155
Good $ense Budget Course Pre-work 157

GOOD $ENSE MINISTRY

CONTENTS

The Pull of the Culture vs. the Mind and Heart of God
The Biblical Financial Principles: Foundation of the Good
   $ense Ministry
Biblical Financial Principles
Benefits of a Good $ense Ministry
Questions and Answers about Implementing a Good $ense Ministry
Removing Common Barriers That Make It Difficult to Speak about
   Money from the Pulpit
Small Groups within Good $ense
Tips for Group Counseling
Good $ense Ministry Proposal
Counseling Procedure

THE PULL OF THE CULTURE VS. THE MIND AND HEART OF GOD

As you begin to implement your Good $ense Ministry, it is important to understand the two opposing forces you will be contending with. Good $ense describes these as the Pull of the Culture and the Mind and Heart of God. These two forces are each trying to gain our allegiance.

The Pull of the Culture

The Pull of the Culture exerts its power through a series of cultural myths that are so commonly held and often repeated that it is not an exaggeration to suggest that we may be victims of brainwashing—that phenomena in which the mind believes something that is untrue simply because it has heard it so often.

The three most common myths are:

- *"Things bring happiness."* We hear the never-ending litany: "Buy me! Wear me! Drive me! Drink me! Put me on your face or in your hair, and you'll find happiness and popularity and fame."

  What a huge lie! There are mountains of evidence to the contrary. If things brought happiness, the United States would be the most blissful nation on the planet, since we have more "stuff" than any other nation. Unfortunately, by many measures, we are not a happy nation. We need only look at current suicide, divorce, and depression statistics to see that we're not a happy nation. In fact, the data seems to suggest there is often an inverse correlation between our material acquisitions and our happiness.

- *"Debt is expected and unavoidable."* Debt in our culture is made to appear glamorous by dressing it up in a tuxedo and calling it "credit." Our culture promotes credit as painless and without negative consequences. Familiar phrases seductively ring in our ears:

  - "Play now, pay later."
  - "No money down. No payments until…"
  - "You can afford it. Minimum payments are only…"
  - "You deserve it."

Many have bought into this myth and the consequences are staggering. According to a recent *Wall Street Journal* report, household borrowing in the U.S. increased 60 percent between 1995 and 2000. In 1999, almost $60 billion was paid in credit card interest alone!

The myth that debt is unavoidable is perpetuated by the fact that it is so encouraged and embraced by our culture. Historically, if you were offered the opportunity to borrow money it was assumed you had the means to repay it. Now with over 3 billion credit card solicitations and 1.4 million bankruptcies per year, that obviously is no longer true.

There are huge negative consequences to debt, both economic and spiritual. People are being crushed by the effect of debt and compound interest working against them, suffering tremendous anxiety and concern over meeting payments. Marriages and relationships are torn apart by the conflict and anxiety created by debt. The borrower really is slave to the lender as debt robs us of our future flexibility and freedom and we mortgage our future on depreciating items that will be used up, worn out, and thrown away before they are paid for.

The spiritual dangers of debt are also huge and include feeding envy and greed, presuming upon an uncertain future, and denying God the opportunity to teach us through providing in his way (rather than our going into debt) or by denying us something we may want but—for his reasons—would not be in our best interest.

- *"A little more money will solve your problems."* The proof this is a myth comes from the research involving people across a wide economic spectrum, including those who made from $20,000 to $200,000 per year. Researchers asked the question, "How much more money would you need to really be okay and ease the financial pressure?"

The answers were consistently just about ten percent more than the person was currently making. Those making $20,000 believed another $2000 would set things right, while those at the $200,000 income level felt an additional $20,000 would do it. The truth, of course, is that until we have learned to manage what we currently make and live within our income, making more will simply allow us to spend more and to continue to feel the need for "just about 10 percent more."

The Mind and Heart of God

Countering the Pull of the Culture is the Mind and Heart of God. The Mind and Heart of God is expressed through a series of Biblical Financial Principles (see pages 77–81).

Unlike the Pull of the Culture, God doesn't shout or plead. In his ever quiet voice, he asks us to be faithful to him. Financial freedom—the contentment we experience as we faithfully manage financial resources according to God's principles and purposes—is the byproduct of that faithfulness. Matthew 6:33 says, "Seek first his kingdom and his righteousness, and all these things will be given to you as well."

In biblical terms, the dilemma created by these two forces can be described as that of one servant and two masters. The Bible makes it clear that we can't serve two masters. Matthew 6:24 says, "No one can serve two masters. For you will hate one and love the other, or be devoted to one and despise the other. You cannot serve both God and money" (NLT). The Good $ense Ministry helps those we serve resist the Pull of the Culture and turn toward the Mind and Heart of God.

THE BIBLICAL FINANCIAL PRINCIPLES: FOUNDATION OF THE GOOD $ENSE MINISTRY

The Good $ense Ministry is founded upon a set of Biblical Financial Principles that express the ministry's beliefs about how the Bible tells us to manage our money.

The overarching and most important of the principles is the cultivation of a steward's mindset. By that, we mean the mindset of one who is managing resources rather than owning them. A modern analogy to that of being a steward would be being a trustee. If you were incapacitated, and someone was made the trustee of your estate, that person would have no rights to those assets that belonged to you, simply the responsibility to manage them in the way that was in your best interest.

In a similar fashion, the Bible makes clear that in the eternal perspective, we own nothing; God has simply entrusted us with resources that ultimately belong to him. Consequently, we are to use them in ways that honor and please him.

The concept of stewardship/trusteeship versus ownership is at the heart of everything the Bible has to say about money and our proper relationship to it.

The remaining Biblical Financial Principles center around the five financial areas of our lives: earning, giving, saving, debt, and spending. These areas represent the usual way in which we get money (earning) and the four things we can do with it once we have it—we can give it away, save it, pay debt with it, or spend it. The Bible is clear and has much to say on each of these topics. We are to be diligent earners, generous givers, wise savers, cautious debtors, and prudent consumers. The biblical basis for this statement appears on the following pages in summary form. A more detailed listing of Biblical Financial Principles is on pages 80–81.

BIBLICAL FINANCIAL PRINCIPLES

Steward's Mindset

We came into the world with nothing, and we will leave the world with nothing. Everything that we have in the interim has been entrusted to us by a loving God who created all things and retained ownership of everything he created. Biblical references include:

- God created everything. (Genesis 1:1)
- God owns everything. (Psalm 24:1; 50:10, 12b)
- We are stewards/trustees. (1 Colossians 4:1-2)

Earning

In Genesis, God invited humankind to join him in the ongoing work of creation. In the process, God established work as a blessing, not as a curse, and gave all work dignity. We are called to work diligently, with purpose, and to be grateful for the gift of our innate intelligence and health which allow us to work and to receive compensation for it.

- Be diligent. (Colossians 3:23)
- Be purposeful. (Colossians 3:23; 1 Timothy 5:8)
- Be grateful. (Deuteronomy 8:18)

Giving

We are made to give. We are created in the image of God, and God is a loving and generous being. Therefore, we will only be fully satisfied when we are sharing with those less fortunate than ourselves. The Bible lists many reasons to give:

- As a response to God's goodness. (James 1:17)
- To focus on God as our source of security. (Matthew 6:19-20a, 23b-33)
- To help achieve economic justice. (Deuteronomy 15;11; 2 Corinthians 8:13–14)
- To bless others. (Genesis 12:2-3)

In addition to the biblical reasons to give, it is evident that the act of giving is the most effective way to break the powerful hold that money can otherwise have on us.

Saving

While we are to depend on God as our ultimate source of security and not on money, the Bible encourages us to plan for the future and for the unexpected by saving wisely. But while it is wise to save for appropriate goals, it is sinful to hoard. To avoid hoarding, we each must come to grips with the question, "When is enough, enough?"

- It is wise to save. (Proverbs 6:8; 21:20)
- It is sinful to hoard. (Luke 12:16-21)

Debt

The Bible is clear that we are to repay our debts, but since the borrower is slave to the lender, it is wiser still to avoid debt.

- Repay debt. (Psalm 37:21)
- Avoid debt. (Proverbs 22:7)

Spending

As Christians, we are called to live with moderation and discipline and to be content with what we have. We must recognize that materialism is a competing theology in which things become idols and greed becomes a driving force.

- Beware of idols. (Deuteronomy 5:8; Romans 1:25)
- Guard against greed. (Luke 12:15)
- Be content. (Philippians 4:12)

See the following pages for a detailed list of Biblical Financial Principles.

BIBLICAL FINANCIAL PRINCIPLES

FOUNDATION OF THE GOOD $ENSE MINISTRY
Cultivate a steward's mindset.

GOD CREATED EVERYTHING
In the beginning there was nothing, and God created (Genesis 1:1).

GOD OWNS EVERYTHING
"The silver is mine and the gold is mine," declares the LORD Almighty" (Haggai 2:8). "Every animal of the forest is mine, and the cattle on a thousand hills" (Psalm 50:10). "The earth is the Lord's, and everything in it. The world and all its people belong to him." Psalm 24:1 NLT).

Flowing out of the fact that God created and owns everything is the logical conclusion that whatever we possess is not really ours, but belongs to God; we are simply entrusted with our possessions. Therefore, we are trustees, not owners. Although 1 Corinthians 4 (quoted below) does not directly refer to material possessions, its counsel is applicable to this aspect of life as well.

WE ARE TRUSTEES
"A person who is put in charge as a manager must be faithful" (1 Corinthians 4:1–2 NLT).

WE CAN'T SERVE TWO MASTERS
"No one can serve two masters. For you will hate one and love the other, or be devoted to one and despise the other. You cannot serve both God and money" (Matthew 6:24 NLT).

USE RESOURCES WISELY
"His master replied, 'Well done, good and faithful servant! You have been faithful with a few things; I will put you in charge of many things. Come and share your master's happiness!'" (Matthew 25:21–28).

PURSUE BIBLICAL, FINANCIAL KNOWLEDGE
"Buy the truth and do not sell it; get wisdom, discipline and understanding" (Proverbs 23:23). "Plans fail for lack of counsel, but with many advisers they succeed" (Proverbs 15:22).

MEASURABLE GOALS AND REALISTIC PLANS
"Commit to the LORD whatever you do, and your plans will succeed" (Proverbs 16:3).

TRUSTWORTHINESS MATTERS
"Whoever can be trusted with very little can also be trusted with much, and whoever is dishonest with very little will also be dishonest with much. So if you have not been trustworthy in handling worldly wealth, who will trust you with true riches? And if you have not been trustworthy with someone else's property, who will give you property of your own?" (Luke 16:10–12).

EARNING
The Diligent Earner—One who produces with diligence and purpose and is content and grateful for what he or she has.

God established work while Adam and Eve were yet in the Garden of Eden. God invited them to join him in the ongoing act of caring for creation. Work before the fall of Adam and Eve is a blessing, not a curse. All work has dignity. Our work should be characterized by the following principles.

BE DILIGENT; SERVE GOD
"Whatever you do, work at it with all your heart, as working for the Lord" (Colossians 3:23).

PROVIDE FOR OURSELVES AND THOSE DEPENDENT ON US
"Those who won't care for their own relatives, especially those living in the same household, have denied what we believe. Such people are worse than unbelievers" (1 Timothy 5:8 NLT).

BE GRATEFUL; REMEMBER FROM WHOM INCOME REALLY COMES
"Remember the LORD your God, for it is he who gives you the ability to produce wealth" (Deuteronomy 8:18).

ENJOY YOUR WORK; BE CONTENT IN IT
"It is good for people to eat well, drink a good glass of wine, and enjoy their work—whatever they do under the sun—for however long God lets them live. And it is a good thing to receive wealth from God and the good health to enjoy it. To enjoy your work and accept your lot in life—that is indeed a gift from God" (Ecclesiastes 5:18-19 NLT).

BE TRANSFORMED WORKERS
"Slaves, obey your earthly masters with respect and fear, and with sincerity of heart, just as you would obey Christ. Obey them not only to win their favor when their eye is on you, but like slaves of Christ, doing the will of God from your heart" (Ephesians 6:5-6).

EARN POTENTIAL, SHARE EXCESS
"If you are a thief, stop stealing. Begin using your hands for honest work, and then give generously to others in need" (Ephesians 4:28 NLT).

GIVING
The Generous Giver—One who gives with an obedient will, a joyful attitude, and a compassionate heart.

WE ARE MADE TO GIVE
We are made in the image of God (Genesis 1:26-27). God is gracious and generous. We will lead a more satisfied and fulfilled life when we give to others.

GIVE AS A RESPONSE TO GOD'S GOODNESS
"Every good and perfect gift is from above" (James 1:17). Therefore, we give out of gratefulness for what we have received.

GIVE TO FOCUS ON GOD AS OUR SOURCE AND SECURITY
"But seek first his kingdom and his righteousness and all these things will be given to you as well" (Matthew 6:33).

GIVE TO HELP ACHIEVE ECONOMIC JUSTICE
"Our desire . . . is that there might be equality. At the present time your plenty will supply what they need" (2 Corinthians 8:13-14). Throughout Scripture, God expresses his concern for the poor and calls us to share with those less fortunate.

GIVE TO BLESS OTHERS
"I will make you into a great nation and I will bless you; I will make your name great, and you will be a blessing. And I will bless you, and make your name great; and so you shall be a blessing" (Genesis 12:2-3). If we are blessed with resources beyond our needs, it is not for the purpose of living more lavishly but to bless others. We are blessed to be a blessing.

BE WILLING TO SHARE
"Command them [the rich] to do good, to be rich in good deeds, and to be generous and willing to share" (1 Timothy 6:18).

GIVE TO BREAK THE HOLD OF MONEY
Another reason to give is that doing so breaks the hold that money might otherwise have on us. While the Bible doesn't specifically say so, it is evident that persons who give freely and generously are not controlled by money but have freedom.

GIVE JOYFULLY, GENEROUSLY, IN A TIMELY MANNER
"Out of the most severe trial, their overflowing joy and their extreme poverty welled up in rich generosity. For I testify that they gave as much as they were able, and even beyond their ability. Entirely on their own, they urgently pleaded with us for the privilege of sharing in this service to the saints" (2 Corinthians 8:1-5).

GIVE WISELY
"We want to avoid any criticism of the way we administer this liberal gift" (2 Corinthians 8:20).

GIVE EXPECTANTLY AND CHEERFULLY
"The one who plants generously will get a generous crop. You must each make up your own mind as to how much you should give. Don't give reluctantly or in response to pressure. For God loves the person who gives cheerfully" (2 Corinthians 9:6-7 NLT; see also verses 10-14).

MOTIVES FOR GIVING ARE IMPORTANT

Unless our motives are right, we can give all we have—even our bodies as sacrifices—and it will be for naught (I Corinthians 13). We can be scrupulous with tithing and still not have the right motives. Jesus rebuked the religious leaders of his day for this very thing: "You hypocrites! You give a tenth of your spices—mint, dill and cummin. But you have neglected the more important matters of the law—justice, mercy and faithfulness" (Matthew 23:23).

SAVING

The Wise Saver—One who builds, preserves, and invests with discernment.

IT IS WISE TO SAVE

"In the house of the wise are stores of choice food and oil, but [the] foolish ... devour all [they have]" (Proverbs 21:20). "Go to the ant, you sluggard; consider its ways and be wise! It has no commander, no overseer or ruler, yet it stores its provisions in summer and gathers its food at harvest" (Proverbs 6:8).

IT IS SINFUL TO HOARD

And he gave them an illustration: "A rich man had a fertile farm that produced fine crops. In fact, his barns were full to overflowing. So he said, 'I know! I'll tear down my barns and build bigger ones. Then I'll have room enough to store everything. And I'll sit back and say to myself, My friend, you have enough stored away for years to come. Now take it easy! Eat, drink, and be merry!' But God said to him, 'You fool! You will die this very night. Then who will get it all?' Yes, a person is a fool to store up earthly wealth but not have a rich relationship with God" (Luke 12:16-21 NLT).

CALCULATE COST; PRIORITIZE

"But don't begin until you count the cost. For who would begin construction of a building without first getting estimates and then checking to see if there is enough money to pay the bills? Otherwise, you might complete only the foundation before running out of funds. And then how everyone would laugh at you! They would say, 'There's the person who started that building and ran out of money before it was finished!'" (Luke 14:28-30 NLT).

AVOID GET-RICH-QUICK SCHEMES

"The trustworthy will get a rich reward. But the person who wants to get rich quick will only get into trouble" (Proverbs 28:20 NLT).

SEEK WISE COUNSELORS

"Let the wise listen and add to their learning, and let the discerning get guidance" (Proverbs 1:5).

ESTABLISH A JOB BEFORE BUYING HOME

"Finish your outdoor work and get your fields ready; after that, build your house" (Proverbs 24:27).

DIVERSIFY YOUR HOLDINGS

"Give portions to seven, yes to eight, for you do not know what disaster will come upon the land" (Ecclesiastes 11:2).

DEBT

The Cautious Debtor—One who avoids entering into debt, is careful and strategic when incurring debt, and always repays debt.

REPAY DEBT AND DO SO PROMPTLY

"The wicked borrow and do not repay, but the righteous give generously" (Psalm 37:21). "Do not say to your neighbor, 'Come back later; I'll give it tomorrow'—when you now have it with you" (Proverbs 3:28).

AVOID THE BONDAGE OF DEBT

"The rich rule over the poor, and the borrower is servant to the lender" (Proverbs 22:7).

DEBT PRESUMES ON THE FUTURE

"Now listen, you who say, 'Today or tomorrow we will go to this or that city, spend a year there, carry on business and make money.' Why, you do not even know what will happen tomorrow. What is your life? You are a mist that appears for a little while and then vanishes" (James 4:13-14).

DEBT CAN DENY GOD THE OPPORTUNITY TO WORK IN OUR LIVES AND TEACH US VALUABLE LESSONS

God may wish to show us his love by providing us with something we desire but for which we have no resources. If we go into debt to get it anyway, we deny him that opportunity (see Luke 12:22-32). In the same way that parents refrain from giving a child everything the child wants because parents know it isn't in the child's best interest, incurring debt can rob God of the opportunity to teach us through denial. Ecclesiastes 7:14 reminds us: "When times are good, be happy; but when times are bad, consider: God has made the one as well as the other."

DEBT CAN FOSTER ENVY AND GREED

"Beware! Don't be greedy for what you don't have. Real life is not measured by how much we own" (Luke 12:15).

GIVE AND PAY WHAT YOU OWE

"Give everyone what you owe them: Pay your taxes and import duties, and give respect and honor to all to whom it is due" (Romans 13:7 NLT).

DON'T CO-SIGN

"Do not co-sign another person's note or put up a guarantee for someone else's loan. If you can't pay it, even your bed will be snatched from under you" (Proverbs 22:26-27 NLT).

DEBT CAN DISRUPT SPIRITUAL GROWTH

"The fruit of the Spirit is love, joy, peace, patience, kindness, goodness, faithfulness, gentleness and self-control. Against such things there is no law" (Galatians 5:22-23).

SPENDING

The Prudent Consumer—One who enjoys the fruits of their labor yet guards against materialism.

BEWARE OF IDOLS

"You shall not make yourself an idol in the form of anything in heaven above or on the earth beneath or in the waters below" (Deuteronomy 5:8). Materialism—which so saturates our culture—is nothing less than a competing theology in which matter (things) is of ultimate significance; that is, things become gods or idols. "They ... worshipped and served created things rather than the Creator" (Romans 1:25).

GUARD AGAINST GREED; THINGS DO NOT BRING HAPPINESS

"Beware! Don't be greedy for what you don't have. Real life is not measured by how much we own" (Luke 12:15).

SEEK MODERATION

"Give me neither poverty nor riches, but give me only my daily bread. Otherwise, I may have too much and disown you and say, 'Who is the LORD?' Or I may become poor and steal, and so dishonor the name of my God" (Proverbs 30:8-9).

BE CONTENT

"I know what it is to be in need, and I know what it is to have plenty. I have learned the secret of being content in any and every situation, whether well fed or hungry, whether living in plenty or in want. I can do everything through him who gives me strength" (Philippians 4:12-13).

"Godliness with contentment is great gain. For we brought nothing into the world, and we can take nothing out of it. But if we have food and clothing, we will be content with that" (1 Timothy 6:6-8).

DON'T WASTE GOD'S RESOURCES

"When they had all had enough to eat, he said to his disciples, 'Gather the pieces that are left over. Let nothing be wasted'" (John 6:12).

ENJOY A PORTION OF GOD'S PROVISION

"Command those who are rich in this present world not to be arrogant nor to put their hope in wealth, which is so uncertain, but to put their hope in God, who richly provides us with everything for our enjoyment. Command them to do good, to be rich in good deeds, and to be generous and willing to share. In this way they will lay up treasure for themselves as a firm foundation for the coming age, so that they may take hold of the life that is truly life" (1 Timothy 6:17-19).

WATCH YOUR FINANCES (BUDGET)

"Be sure you know the condition of your flocks, give careful attention to your herds; for riches do not endure forever, and a crown is not secure for all generations" (Proverbs 27:23-24).

BENEFITS OF A GOOD $ENSE MINISTRY

There are numerous benefits of a Good $ense Ministry. The following pages highlight just a few of them.

"Give careful thought to [our] ways"

We live in a nation of unprecedented wealth. Much of what we now consider necessities were not available to even the wealthiest people in the world 100 years ago. We are busy; we are productive; always on the move; always on the go. Yet, we are never content, we cannot produce and consume enough to satisfy our insatiable appetites. Perhaps it is time that we "give careful thought to [our] ways" (Haggai 1:5-6).

One of the benefits of the Good $ense Ministry is that it will allow us to "give careful thought to [our] ways."

- How our ways have been influenced by the foolish myths of our culture
- How God is calling us to faithfully manage our resources
- How we can use practical tools to manage the resources God has given us in ways that honor him

Stopping Idolatry

In our materialistic society, it becomes very easy to let money and things take precedence in our lives. When this happens, we have elevated those things to a position above God and, in so doing, have made them the gods of our lives (Matthew 6:24). We have replaced our love of God with a love for money and opened ourselves to all kinds of evil (1 Timothy 6:10).

The Good $ense Ministry will keep us alert to these areas of temptation and deception and, as a result, will make it easier to resist them and to act in accordance with the Mind and Heart of God. The Bible tells us that the wise seek counsel before making decisions. Good $ense counselors give the church a group of wise and knowledgeable people from whom others can seek counsel.

Reaching Out Evangelistically

The *Good $ense Budget Course* and the counseling ministry can be opened up to those outside the church and, as they are pointed to ways to correct their budgets and debt problems, the ministry can become a springboard to point them to the One who holds control of all those resources.

Helping the Poor

Perhaps your church has a benevolence program. Many people using such a program could benefit from Christian budget and debt reduction counseling. To paraphrase the popular saying, rather than simply giving the person a fish, the Good $ense Ministry approach would teach them to fish. While the person may still need temporary assistance from the church, they can be taught to utilize their funds most effectively and guided to become self-sufficient in the long term.

A Good $ense Ministry can also help the benevolence program of a church to understand if the request represents true need. This allows the church to be a better steward of the resources allocated to assist others.

Strengthening Marriages

The percentages vary somewhat depending on their source, but all those knowledgeable about such things agree that at least a majority of marital conflict centers around money. A Good $ense Ministry provides the teaching and practical tools that strengthen many marriages.

Increasing Resources Available for Ministry

Though not a primary reason for a Good $ense Ministry, the reality is that as people understand the biblical wisdom concerning money management, and as they manage their resources better, they will increase their giving to the church, which will provide the church additional resources for ministry.

Summary

Money is a huge issue of life for each one of us. A majority of our waking hours are spent either making it, spending it, worrying about it, fighting over it, or protecting it—and it is an area in which all of us are susceptible to temptation and failure. For many of us, money is the chief rival god. The Good $ense Ministry provides the teaching, the training, and the encouragement and support to "give careful thought to [our] ways" and to follow the Mind and Heart of God rather than succumb to the Pull of the Culture.

QUESTIONS AND ANSWERS ABOUT IMPLEMENTING A GOOD $ENSE MINISTRY

Will people come to a *Good $ense Budget Course*?

We must admit, budgeting is not on the top of most people's list of favorite subjects. Many people are very tense and uptight about this subject. Those in financial crisis would rather ignore the topic. Many of those not feeling any financial pressure consider the topic unnecessary.

The success of the *Good $ense Budget Course* depends on many factors and attendance at the initial offering varies widely. One church has a membership of 900 and had 400 show up to their first *Good $ense Budget Course*. While you may not experience the same level of response, experience has shown that people do attend and that generally attendance grows the second and third times the course is offered.

One key factor that will affect attendance is the support of the church leaders, especially the senior pastor. When a senior pastor becomes engaged in actively and openly supporting the program, the results are usually greater than anticipated. In addition, it is important to publicize that the course is for everyone, not just those in financial difficulty. The course offers important insights into what the Bible says about one's relationship to money that are helpful to those who already manage money well. And it provides affirmation and encouragement to those who are living in accord with Biblical Financial Principles.

Should the church be talking about money? After all, it is a rather secular subject and not very spiritual.

The fact is that money is a recurring underlying spiritual topic. The Bible contains some 2,300 verses about money and possessions, a majority of Jesus' parables were about how we relate to our money and our stuff, and 15 percent of all of Jesus' recorded words had to do with money.

Failure to teach our people about money is failing to teach them one of the key issues that keep men and women from becoming fully devoted followers of Christ. Failure to teach our people about money is failing to recognize the hold that money can have on the hearts, the lives, and the actions of God's people. Failure to teach our people about money is failing to preach and teach the whole counsel of God. We do not want to stand before God some day and try to answer why we neglected a topic that God deems so important.

Our church is known as a seeker-friendly church. Won't talking about money the way the Bible does, scare seekers away?

Most of the "turn off" that people—committed members as well as seekers—feel over the church talking about money is because the talk is most often about giving and comes at the time of the annual stewardship drive or some budgetary crisis.

The reality, of course, is that the Bible speaks about money in many more contexts than just giving—as important as that is. And many of those contexts are very "seeker friendly" and speak to the very issues that seekers are most concerned about.

For example, the thing most seekers are seeking is meaning and purpose and the answer to the question, "What is life really all about?" Many seekers have sought this answer where the world has indicated meaning and purpose are found—in things—in the stuff that money can buy. If a pastor were to announce that a person's life does not consist in the abundance of their possessions (Luke 12:15), most seekers would probably respond, "I agree. Been there, done that. So what does life consist of?" A message that followed and explained how money and things do not provide the happiness and security they so often promise but that a life committed to Christ does, could provide the ultimate answer to the questions the seeker is raising.

Numerous other examples can be found in the audio tape messages listed on page 123. Messages that were given at seeker services are so indicated. Message tapes, transcripts, and other programming resources are also listed and can be purchased by calling (800) 570-9812 or by logging on to www.willowcreek.com.

Won't people be reluctant to reveal their personal finances to a counselor who is a fellow church member?

Finances have long been a very private matter within our culture and there may be hesitancy on the part of some to seek counsel, especially in the early stages of your ministry. One way to affirm the value of transparency and humility around this issue is to preach and teach on how secrecy and evasion are not supported by Scripture. It may also be helpful to reference the truth of this principle in other areas of life. For example, if a person had mechanical trouble or a question about their car, they would be very inclined to turn to a friend who is a mechanic specially trained to address such situations. Why not do likewise with difficulties or questions about finances?

Over time, an even more significant factor in encouraging people to take advantage of counseling services will be the testimonies of those whose lives have been changed because of the help, encouragement, and hope they received from the ministry.

Will counseling people about their finances open up the church to potential liabilities?

While it is true that any service or ministry offered by a church has the potential to lead to a lawsuit, the only alternative is to do nothing—in which case, someone would probably sue for that! The key here is that counselors are trained and clearly understand their role as budget counselors rather than financial planners.

There is also a disclaimer on the last page of the Client Profile that clients read and agree to when they sign the form. If a disgruntled client decides to file a lawsuit, this provides documentation that the ministry clearly communicated—and the client understood—the expectations and goals of Good $ense counseling.

How can we keep the ministry from being perceived as one more way to get people to give more money to the church?

First, be sure senior church leadership is clear on this point and that giving is not unduly stressed in messages from the pulpit that precede Good $ense events.

Second, be strategic about how the ministry is positioned organizationally. It is best not to align the Good $ense Ministry with the church finance committee/department. Instead, it should be placed on the ministry side of the organizational chart.*

Finally, affirm the core teaching of the Good $ense materials themselves. Rather than focusing primarily on giving, Good $ense emphasizes spiritual formation by understanding and applying the Mind and Heart of God.

What can we say to someone who adamantly insists the church should not talk about money?

Welcome the dialogue, knowing that all the biblical support is on your side! Ask them why they feel this way and follow up by asking if they can help you understand their position from a biblical perspective. Invite them to watch with you and then discuss the *Casting a Vision for Good $ense* video. With sensitivity to their concerns, explain that you do not see how the whole Word of God can be effectively taught without speaking to this topic. Point out how much many people need training to handle their finances wisely and how the Bible is full of such wisdom.

---

* This is not to imply that properly handling church finances is not a ministry—it is.

REMOVING COMMON BARRIERS THAT MAKE IT DIFFICULT TO SPEAK ABOUT MONEY FROM THE PULPIT

Money is a huge life issue. Its impact upon us is inescapable, and our relationship to it has very significant spiritual ramifications. Jesus talked about money a great deal. Yet, most pastors treat money as the great silent subject. Let's explore some of the reasons pastors tend to be hesitant to talk about money.

We're not taught how to talk about money.

According to research done by the Christian Stewardship Association, less than 10 percent of seminaries have a course on stewardship and many of those are not required. So initially, many ministers lack teaching and training on a subject that is the second most mentioned one in all of Scripture.

We have a natural inclination to not be interested in money.

If money was of significant interest or importance, chances are we wouldn't be in the ministry! The combination of not being very interested in it and not knowing much about it from a biblical standpoint (back to our first point) leads naturally to an inclination to not saying much about it.

There tends to be a feeling that it's self-serving to talk about money.

After all, our salaries come from the money people give to the church, so to talk about money could make it seem like we were just worried about our own interests. This attitude comes in large measure from equating talking about money with talking about giving—a not uncommon, but very erroneous conclusion. Talking about money from a biblical perspective includes giving, but that is only one small part of the much larger picture.

For some of us, it's hard to preach and teach with integrity when our own finances are a mess.

Sometimes, for understandable reasons, some of us struggle with the biblical directives to be generous in our giving, to save for the unexpected, to avoid consumer debt, to be content and live within our means, and therefore find it difficult to challenge others to do so. The obvious but not always easy antidote is to take the steps to get whatever help is necessary to correct the situation. It's not necessary to be at a place of perfection, but for integrity's sake, we have to be moving in the right direction.

We tend to be intimidated by the topic of money and by those who have a lot of it.

Given the importance that money and the possession of it is given by our culture, it's easy—particularly for those of us who have not been taught about it and who have very little interest in it—to feel very inadequate and intimidated by those who have money. What is a proven fact, however, is that those with a lot of money often feel very isolated, have significant pastoral needs, and are, in fact, in grave spiritual danger because of the power that money can have over them. The recognition of the pastoral opportunities in this area should serve to counteract our intimidation.

People may get upset if we talk about money.

Chances are that some will, but that should never be the rationale for our deciding what biblical truths our people need to hear. In some cases, where we have only talked about money in the context of giving to the annual budget and done so with a guilt-producing approach, it may be appropriate for people to be upset. But when scriptural truth about money and our relationship to it is properly presented and results in a person being upset, that is an indictment, not of our teaching, but of the person's spiritual condition and presents a wonderful pastoral opportunity. The statement, "I'm sorry the message was upsetting to you. Can you help me understand why you feel we shouldn't talk about money in the church?" and the subsequent conversation in which we have the opportunity to point out how often Jesus talked about money and the biblical basis for our message, can be life changing for the individual.

We may tend to be hesitant to talk about money because the evil one doesn't want us to.

There has been a historic feud between God and money, and money is clearly the chief rival god in many people's lives. An improper relationship to our money is a huge barrier to our relationship with God, and the devil would like nothing better than for us to avoid the topic and let the pull of our culture and materialism hold sway in people's lives. So we can be sure that Satan will play upon any of our own natural hesitancy to hold us back from speaking God's truth in this arena. Let's not be guilty of so doing.

Pages 123–127 list Recommended Resources, including message transcripts, drama scripts, and other resources that may be helpful in planning services.

SMALL GROUPS WITHIN GOOD $ENSE

Small groups are an integral part of the Good $ense Ministry structure. They are particularly important since the serving portion of the ministry is done "solo," is often difficult, and always places the counselor or teacher at the heart of deep spiritual conflict.

Biblically functioning small groups should contain three components: learning, loving, and doing. The learning component is about discovering (intellectual knowledge) and making the truths of God's Word part of our lives (experiential knowledge). The loving part is about accountability, about the support necessary to be transformed from the world and conformed to the image of Jesus Christ. The doing component is showing our faith by our works, putting our faith into practice.

There are several types of small groups that can be utilized by a Good $ense Ministry to help men and women grow in their financial faithfulness. These include new counselor groups, experienced counselor groups, study groups, and counseling groups.

New Counselor Group

This is for counselors who have just completed the *Good $ense Counselor Training Workshop.*

Purpose of the Group
- To serve as a place where counselors can continue to practice their skills in a safe and non-threatening environment
- To provide the support needed to complete their first cases
- To deepen their understanding of the principles of biblical stewardship—to apply them to their personal lives—to incorporate them in their counseling
- To learn the important place that prayer has in the success of the Good $ense Ministry

Leadership of the Group
Ideally, the leader is an experienced Good $ense counselor. Of course, this will not be possible when starting a Good $ense Ministry. Another

option would be to have the leadership come from a core team member or a Good $ense teacher.

Time Frame

Initial group meets for six months—at least once per month—one and one-half to two hours per meeting.

Meeting Content

- Stewardship study (about twenty minutes). This time is a discussion of individual study done during the preceding weeks for the purpose of more deeply understanding biblical stewardship. This could be in the form of Bible study or the use of a resource like Randy Alcorn's book, *Money, Possessions, and Eternity,* which has study guide questions at the end of each chapter.
- Case experience (sixty minutes). This time would be used for counselors to discuss their cases and share concerns about issues they are encountering. If cases have not yet been assigned, this time could be used for additional training and role play of potential cases.
- Prayer (about twenty minutes). A suggested format would be to use this as a time when prayer requests are shared, with each person recording the requests and committing to pray for those requests on a regular basis. End the time with shared prayer.

Experienced Counselor Group

After six months, the new counselor group can shift its focus somewhat as it becomes an ongoing group of experienced counselors.

Purpose of the Group

- To provide encouragement, fellowship, and a sense of belonging in the ministry
- To grow in understanding and living out biblical stewardship
- To hold each other accountable for the spiritual growth of their clients

Leadership of the Group

The leadership of this group could be one of the counselors in the group, a Good $ense teacher, or a core team member.

Time Frame

This is an open-ended group and would be meeting at least once per month. The length of the meeting would be about two hours. The group may consider meeting around a meal to help build the community component.

Meeting Content

- Learning (one hour). This group can continue to go deeper into their understanding of biblical stewardship. They may expand their study to include topics such as counseling skills or spiritual disciplines. The key goal of this part of the time together is continued spiritual growth.
- Mutual assistance (forty-five minutes). Counsel and advice regarding situations they are encountering in their cases.
- Prayer (fifteen minutes). Prayer for each other both as counselors and as brothers and sisters in Christ; prayer for their clients and for the church.

Study Group

This is for people who have completed a *Good $ense Budget Course.*

Purpose of the Group

To delve deeper into a study of one or more of the uses of money (earning, giving, saving, debt, or spending) or some other specific topic following the *Good $ense Budget Course.*

Leadership of the Group

The leader should be a Good $ense teacher or knowledgeable counselor.

Time Frame

Varies depending on the topic chosen by the group.

Meeting Content

- Cultural perspective. What are the influences on our thinking?
- Biblical teaching. What is the perspective from God's viewpoint?
- Practical application (topic dependent). Examples include how to prepare a budget, how to develop a Debt Reduction Plan, how to shop

more carefully, how to give more responsibly, etc., pertaining to the specific topic of study.

The focus is to give additional information, correct a specific problem(s) the members have with financial management, or to help them take action in a specific area.

Counseling Group

This is a special group for red-case clients who select the option of engaging in the counseling process in a group setting rather than one-on-one. While many clients will opt for one-on-one counseling, a surprising number of clients are willing to receive counsel in the context of a small group. Sometimes such a group will evolve out of relationships developed around the tables at the *Good $ense Budget Course.* While every client's situation is unique, there are also similarities that allow for a group approach. For example, everyone needs to develop a budget, learn to track expenses, create a Debt Reduction Plan, etc.

Purpose of the Group

To complete the counseling process while experiencing the camaraderie and support of other group members.

Benefits of Group Counseling

Although the administration and coordination of such an approach is more complex, there are some significant benefits:

- The use of counselors is leveraged. Two counselors can accommodate a group of five or six clients versus one counselor serving one client.
- The members of the group can act as accountability and encouragement for one another and, as such, add a powerful supplement to the efforts of the counselors.
- The counselors learn from one another as they work together and compliment one another's strengths.
- Unlike the situation in which a one-on-one client fails to show up for an appointment and the counselor's time is wasted, if one group member is unable to come at the last minute, the other members of the group can still provide a productive use of counselor's time.

Leadership of the Group

The leadership should be two Good $ense counselors who are comfortable engaging in small group counseling. This could be a good opportunity for a newer counselor to learn from a more experienced one. See pages 97–98 for tips on group counseling.

Time Frame

This type of group initially commits to meeting for six months and then may choose to continue as a support group, independent of their counselors.

Meeting Content

- Counseling. Coverage of the steps in the counseling process with group input. This comprises a majority of the time.
- Sharing. Group member discussion of successes and concerns.
- Prayer. Prayer for all group members.

From time to time during a meeting, it may be appropriate for one of the counselors to work one-on-one with a client on a particular matter. At such a time, the other counselor would continue the group meeting.

TIPS FOR GROUP COUNSELING

There are a number of important considerations in group counseling. These include clarifying expectations, working as a team, and building credibility and rapport.

Clarifying Expectations in a Group Setting

- Explain that confidentiality is very important. What is shared by members of the group is not to go outside the group under any circumstances.
- The meetings will start on time. Being on time is a way of honoring others in the group.
- Unsolicited advice, faultfinding, and criticizing of self or other group members has no place in the group.
- Opportunity will be given for all members to ask questions.

Working as a Team

- You and your fellow counselor are a team, not competitors for the group's attention or acclaim.
- Function as a "tag team." Play off each other's strengths. When one is speaking, the other should observe the group and be ready to supplement what has been said or interject appropriately.
- Have fun as well as deal seriously with the responsibility God has given you with these clients. Appropriate, sensitive humor can help the group work well together. But be careful. Hurt feelings can cripple the group.
- Learn from each other. Be alert to how that can most productively occur. Rest assured you don't know it all yet!
- Prepare together beforehand. Be clear on your goals for the meeting, the time frame, and have clarity regarding your respective assignments. Be sure there is flexibility built into your plans so you can adequately deal with situations as they arise.
- Open and close in prayer.

Building Credibility and Rapport

- As in one-on-one counseling, building rapport is key to ultimately helping the client. In this case you are not only building your personal rapport, but also you are attempting to create an environment in which the group is building relationships with each other.
- Building your rapport and credibility with the group is similar to one-on-one counseling (e.g., self disclosure, how and why you became a counselor, showing an interest in them, being a good listener, etc.).
- At the initial meeting, give the clients an opportunity to share about themselves, why they are in the group, etc. This is important for them to begin to build rapport with one another.
- Do not favor one client(s) over another by giving them more attention. Keep in mind that one of your roles is to rein in the gregarious group member so they do not monopolize time and attention and draw out the shy member so they participate and feel a part of the group.
- Share with the group that one of your hopes is that they will be an encouragement and support to one another. However, be careful to not let the group feel burdened by this expectation. Your hopes will be realized naturally if the group is working well.

GOOD $ENSE MINISTRY PROPOSAL

(Strategic Plan)

This example illustrates how the Good $ense vision can relate to the overall church vision and how the two might be presented in the context of a proposal to senior church leadership.

Vision of Our Church

To establish a safe home for God's people to mature and be equipped as followers of Christ in order to establish an effective mission to non-kingdom people. To bring our community into an encounter with the kingdom of God so that our moral, social, educational, and political structures can be transformed.

Vision of Our Good $ense Ministry

Vision Statement

That every person experience the spiritual, emotional, and relational freedom and joy that results from practicing biblically based stewardship.

Mission Statement

To honor God by educating people about the Biblical Financial Principles of money management and to train and encourage them in the practical, daily application of those principles.

Strategies

- To present courses that educate people on Biblical Financial Principles and train them on how they can apply these principles to their lives.
- To provide free, confidential, budget counseling services to those who need one-on-one assistance and encouragement with their finances.

Benefits

- More openness to the presence of God, and the facilitation of spiritual growth and formation by removing money as the chief rival god.
- Reduced stress in the lives of our people. As the crush of consumer debt is reduced, conflict in marriages lessens and contentment increases.
- Increased giving to the church.
- Increased opportunity for our church to impact our community.

GOOD $ENSE MINISTRY PROPOSAL
Page 2

Overview of Plans

1. Initially offer a one-day *Good $ense Budget Course* to all those who are interested.

2. Offer counseling services to *Good $ense Budget Course* attendees who desire additional assistance.

3. Offer additional opportunities to attend the *Good $ense Budget Course* through our weekly evening adult education classes.

4. Open up budget counseling services to all who desire assistance, not just those who attended the *Good $ense Budget Course.*

5. Offer the *Good $ense Budget Course,* additional courses on other financial topics, and counseling services to the community at large to begin to bring them into an encounter with God.

6. Establish partnerships with other ministries in the church and integrate the Biblical Financial Principles as applicable.

How a Good $ense Ministry Supports the Ministry of the Church

Good $ense helps create the safe haven we desire for our people. It helps eliminate stress and anxiety among those who are burdened with debt, living from paycheck to paycheck, or are managing their finances well but not aware of what a God-honoring lifestyle is. Money is the second most-frequently mentioned topic in the Bible, so we need to open up this area of communication for our people to truly mature and be equipped as followers of Christ.

Good $ense will facilitate increased giving to the church. This provides additional resources for the church to fulfill its mission.

Good $ense provides an entryway into our church for non-believers, since wise financial management is a topic that is relevant to everyone.

Good $ense can impact our community by exposing the powerful cultural myths that lead people to a materialistic, rather than God-honoring, lifestyle.

GOOD $ENSE MINISTRY PROPOSAL
Page 3

Resource Requirements

Volunteer Positions

1   ministry champion (filled)
6   core team members (5 are filled—seeking a bilingual member)
1   Good $ense administrator (may be a core team member initially)
10 counselors (will need to expand to more as ministry expands)
2   teachers (may be core team members initially)

Office Space

Workstation for the Good $ense administrator

Equipment

Laptop computer for presentations and other administrative functions
Phone with voice mail
File cabinets that can be locked

Budget

$ ____ travel (church visits) $ ____ training supplies
$ ____ training materials $ ____ refreshments
$ ____ publicity $ ____ celebrations
$ ____ office supplies $ ____ **Total**

Publicity

The initial course offerings will be tied in with a series of sermons on our relationship to money and will be announced from the pulpit. In addition, advertising will be in the bulletin and on posters throughout the church. When the course is opened up to the public, the congregation will be encouraged to invite a friend and advertising will be done in the local newspaper.

Course Format

The initial *Good $ense Budget Course* will be presented in a one-day workshop format. Subsequent courses will be offered through the adult education weeknight offerings in a six-week format and as one-day workshops.

GOOD $ENSE MINISTRY PROPOSAL
Page 4

Timeline for Implementation

Recruit counselors	September
Set up the Good $ense Ministry office	September
Train Good $ense teachers	September
Select and train Good $ense counselors	November
Set up counseling teams	November
Communicate the Good $ense Ministry vision to the congregation and promote the *Good $ense Budget Course* (early January)	January
Teach the *Good $ense Budget Course* (late January)	January
Offer counseling services	February
Evaluate the *Good $ense Budget Course* and counseling services	February
Hold a "thank you" celebration	March
Implement ministry improvements	March
Select and train additional counselors	April
Offer the *Good $ense Budget Course* to congregation in a six-week format	April
Offer the *Good $ense Budget Course* in one-day format, including those outside the church	September
Develop plan for further expansion	September

Unique Concerns

Due to the large Spanish-speaking population in our community, we may need to also offer our courses and counseling in Spanish. We will consider how to best approach this as we develop our plan for further expansion. In the short-term, we are in the process of adding one bilingual core team member.

COUNSELING PROCEDURE

1. The client contacts the Good $ense office and secures a Client Profile and explanation sheet.

2. The client completes the Client Profile and submits it back to the Good $ense office.

3. The Good $ense administrator reviews the Client Profile and assigns a counselor. Factors such as the nature of the case (positive or negative cash flow), severity of the financial situation, the age, gender, marital status, and profession of the client, and previous counseling history (if any) are taken into consideration when matching clients to counselors. The client's completed Client Profile is given to the counselor. A copy is made for the administrator's file. If a counselor is not immediately available, the client is contacted and told how soon one is anticipated to be available.

4. The counselor calls the client within forty-eight hours of receiving the Client Profile and arranges the first meeting.

5. The counselor completes a Client Progress Report for each meeting and a Case Completion Report when the case is closed. All paperwork is forwarded to the Good $ense administrator when a case is complete and filed appropriately by the administrator.

APPENDIX

PERSONNEL/POSITIONS

CONTENTS

Sample Position Description for Ministry Champion
Sample Position Description for Core Team Members
Sample Position Description for Administrator
Sample Position Description for Teacher
Sample Position Description for Counselor
Sample Position Description for Group Leader
Sample Invitation to Core Team Members
Qualifications of a Good $ense Teacher
Qualifications of a Good $ense Counselor
Interview Outline for Teachers
Interview Outline for Counselors

SAMPLE POSITION DESCRIPTION FOR MINISTRY CHAMPION

MINISTRY POSITION DESCRIPTION

POSITION TITLE
Ministry Champion

MINISTRY
Good $ense

Responsibilities
Communicate the Good $ense vision.
Lead the core team.
Act as a liason for the Good $ense Ministry to serve church leadership.
Enlist volunteers.
Organize training and counseling.

Spiritual Gifts
Leadership   Wisdom
Administration
Discernment

Spiritual Maturity
Leading / guiding

Availability ☒ Flexible

Mon.	Tues.	Wed.	Thur.	Fri.	Sat.	Sun.

Passion for
Helping every believer experience and live a God-honoring financial lifestyle

Personal Style
Energized ☒ People-Oriented
           ☒ Task-Oriented
Organized ☒ Structured
           ☐ Unstructured

Talents/Skills/Abilities
Ability to handle a variety of organizational, administrative, and interpersonal problems. Models the principles of good stewardship.*

Regular Commitments
Weekly core team meetings. Frequent training events/other meetings.

Length of Commitment
2 years

Additional Comments
May not sell or profit from a product or service they can offer to an individual or family they are personally working with or have come in contact with as a result of functioning under the Good $ense Ministry.

Location
☒ Church   ☐ Home   ☒ Other:

Special Notes
Membership required

*Living on a budget; eliminating and not incurring consumer debt; giving cheerfully, regularly, and proportionally; achieving savings goals; and living a moderate lifestyle.

SAMPLE POSITION DESCRIPTION FOR CORE TEAM MEMBERS

MINISTRY POSITION DESCRIPTION

POSITION TITLE
Core Team Member

MINISTRY
Good $ense

Responsibilities
Assist the ministry champion in preparing and presenting the Good $ense Ministry vision and proposal.
Oversee and participate in the implementation process.
Oversee ongoing leadership of the ministry.

Passion for
Helping every believer experience and live a God-honoring financial lifestyle

Personal Style
Energized ☒ People-Oriented
☐ Task-Oriented
Organized ☒ Structured
☒ Unstructured

Spiritual Gifts
Team members should have a variety of gifts.

Talents/Skills/Abilities
A team of individuals with the following backgrounds is ideal: Adult education, counseling, budgeting or finance, communications, and administration. Models the principles of good stewardship*

Spiritual Maturity

Regular Commitments
Weekly core team meetings
Frequent training events / other meetings

Availability ☒ Flexible

Mon.	Tues.	Wed.	Thur.	Fri.	Sat.	Sun.

Length of Commitment
2 years

Additional Comments
May not sell or profit from a product or service they can offer to an individual or family they are personally working with or have come in contact with as a result of functioning under the Good $ense Ministry.

Location
☒ Church ☐ Home ☒ Other:

Special Notes
Membership required

*Living on a budget; eliminating and not incurring consumer debt; giving cheerfully, regularly, and proportionally; achieving savings goals; and living a moderate lifestyle.

SAMPLE POSITION DESCRIPTION FOR ADMINISTRATOR

MINISTRY POSITION DESCRIPTION

POSITION TITLE
Administrator

MINISTRY
Good $ense

Responsibilities
Coordinate the administrative functions of the Good $ense Ministry.
Match clients with counselors.
Organize training course registrations.

Passion for
Helping every believer experience and live a God-honoring financial lifestyle

Personal Style
Energized ☐ People-Oriented
           ☒ Task-Oriented
Organized ☒ Structured
           ☐ Unstructured

Spiritual Gifts
Administration

Talents/Skills/Abilities
Ability to organize forms, files, and procedures
Word processing skills
Models the principles of good stewardship*

Spiritual Maturity
Stable / growing

Regular Commitments
Occasional meetings

Availability ☒ Flexible

Mon.	Tues.	Wed.	Thur.	Fri.	Sat.	Sun.

Length of Commitment
1 year

Additional Comments
May not sell or profit from a product or service they can offer to an individual or family they are personally working with or have come in contact with as a result of functioning under the Good $ense Ministry.

Location
☒ Church   ☐ Home   ☒ Other:

Special Notes
Membership required

*Living on a budget; eliminating and not incurring consumer debt; giving cheerfully, regularly, and proportionally; achieving savings goals; and living a moderate lifestyle.

SAMPLE POSITION DESCRIPTION FOR TEACHER

MINISTRY POSITION DESCRIPTION

POSITION TITLE
Teacher

MINISTRY
Good $ense

Responsibilities
Prepare for and deliver Good $ense Budget Course and/or Good $ense Counselor Training Workshop as well as other Good $ense courses

Spiritual Gifts
Teaching

Spiritual Maturity
Stable/growing

Availability ☒ Flexible

Mon.	Tues.	Wed.	Thur.	Fri.	Sat.	Sun.

Passion for
Helping every believer experience and live a God-honoring financial lifestyle

Personal Style
Energized ☒ People-Oriented
☒ Task-Oriented
Organized ☒ Structured
☐ Unstructured

Talents/Skills/Abilities
Presentation, facilitation, and organizational skills
Models the principles of good stewardship*

Regular Commitments
Courses several times a year

Length of Commitment
1 year

Additional Comments
May not sell or profit from a product or service they can offer to an individual or family they are personally working with or have come in contact with as a result of functioning under the Good $ense Ministry.

Location
☒ Church   ☐ Home   ☒ Other:

Special Notes
Membership required

*Living on a budget; eliminating and not incurring consumer debt; giving cheerfully, regularly, and proportionally; achieving savings goals; and living a moderate lifestyle.

SAMPLE POSITION DESCRIPTION FOR COUNSELOR

MINISTRY POSITION DESCRIPTION

POSITION TITLE
Budget Counselor

MINISTRY
Good $ense

Responsibilities
One-on-one budget counseling

Passion for
Helping every believer experience and live a God-honoring financial lifestyle

Personal Style
Energized ☒ People-Oriented
☒ Task-Oriented
Organized ☒ Structured
☐ Unstructured

Spiritual Gifts
Discernment
Encouragement
Wisdom

Talents/Skills/Abilities
Relational skills
Budgeting experience
Models the principles of good stewardship*

Spiritual Maturity
Stable/growing

Regular Commitments
Counseling sessions every other week
Monthly group meetings
Occasional training events/meetings

Availability ☒ Flexible

Mon.	Tues.	Wed.	Thur.	Fri.	Sat.	Sun.

Length of Commitment
1 year

Additional Comments
May not sell or profit from a product or service they can offer to an individual or family they are personally working with or have come in contact with as a result of functioning under the Good $ense Ministry.

Location
☒ Church   ☐ Home   ☒ Other:

Special Notes
Membership required.

*Living on a budget; eliminating and not incurring consumer debt; giving cheerfully, regularly, and proportionally; achieving savings goals; and living a moderate lifestyle.

SAMPLE POSITION DESCRIPTION FOR GROUP LEADER

MINISTRY POSITION DESCRIPTION

POSITION TITLE
Group Leader

MINISTRY
Good $ense

Responsibilities
One-on-one budget counseling
Facilitate counselor (and/or teacher) group meetings

Passion for
Helping every believer experience and live a God-honoring financial lifestyle

Personal Style
Energized ☒ People-Oriented
☒ Task-Oriented
Organized ☒ Structured
☐ Unstructured

Spiritual Gifts
Leadership
Discernment
Wisdom

Talents/Skills/Abilities
Facilitation skills
Models the principles of good stewardship*

Spiritual Maturity
Stable/growing

Regular Commitments
Monthly group meetings

Availability ☒ Flexible

Mon.	Tues.	Wed.	Thur.	Fri.	Sat.	Sun.

Length of Commitment
1 year

Additional Comments
May not sell or profit from a product or service they can offer to an individual or family they are personally working with or have come in contact with as a result of functioning under the Good $ense Ministry.

Location
☒ Church ☐ Home ☒ Other:

Special Notes
Membership required

*Living on a budget; eliminating and not incurring consumer debt; giving cheerfully, regularly, and proportionally; achieving savings goals; and living a moderate lifestyle.

SAMPLE INVITATION TO CORE TEAM MEMBERS

Good $ense Ministry

[date]

[Name of potential core team member]
[Street address]
[City,] [State] [Zip code]

Dear [name of potential core team member],

I am delighted to invite you to join the [church name] Good $ense Ministry core team. I was so pleased to experience your enthusiasm and excitement for this ministry during our meeting last week. I can't wait for you to meet the other team members who share your passion for biblical financial management.

Our team will meet on [day of the week] from [beginning time] to [ending time]. Our first meeting is [day of the week, date], in [location]. We will get to know each other better, discuss the commitment required for this position, begin to plan for implementing a Good $ense Ministry, and learn more about the Biblical Financial Principles.

Please call me by [date] at [phone number] to confirm your attendance.

I look forward to beginning this important journey with you!

Sincerely,

[Name of ministry champion]
Good $ense Ministry Champion
[Street address]
[City,] [State] [Zip code]

QUALIFICATIONS OF A GOOD $ENSE TEACHER

A Good $ense teacher must be a Christian. He or she must have a growing personal relationship with Jesus Christ and should depend solely on the person of Jesus Christ for salvation.

A Good $ense teacher consistently models in his/her life the principles of good stewardship which undergird the ministry. For example, each teacher should be living on a budget. Their financial life need not be totally free from past financial errors, but should be one that is moving toward responsible Christian goals.

A Good $ense teacher must prepare by thoroughly reading the Leader's Guide, holding practice sessions with other teachers or core team members, reading other resources to deepen one's understanding of Biblical Financial Principles, and visiting another church to experience a course (if practical).

A Good $ense teacher must agree to faithfully serve the ministry within the format designed by its leaders, as well as agree to teach in a manner consistent with the Biblical Financial Principles outlined by Good $ense.

A Good $ense teacher must be willing to receive and act upon constructive feedback provided by the ministry leadership and by participant evaluations.

A Good $ense teacher may not sell or profit from a product or service he or she can offer to an individual or family he or she is personally working with or have come in contact with as a result of serving under the Good $ense Ministry.

QUALIFICATIONS OF A GOOD $ENSE COUNSELOR

A Good $ense counselor must be a Christian. He or she must have a growing personal relationship with Jesus Christ and should depend solely on the person of Jesus Christ for salvation.

A Good $ense counselor is one who has identified his/her gifts and has had those gifts affirmed by others.

A Good $ense counselor consistently models in his/her life the principles of good stewardship which undergird the ministry. For example, each counselor should be living on a budget. The counselor's financial life need not be totally free from past financial errors, but should be one that is moving toward responsible Christian goals.

A Good $ense counselor must attend and complete the *Good $ense Counselor Training Workshop*. Prior to the course, counselors are to read the pre-reading section of the *Good $ense Counselor Training Workshop* Participant's Guide and Manual.

A Good $ense counselor must agree to faithfully serve the ministry within the format designed by its leaders, as well as agree to teach and counsel his/her clients in a manner consistent with the Biblical Financial Principles outlined by Good $ense.

A Good $ense counselor may not sell or profit from a product or service he or she can offer to an individual or family he or she is personally working with or have come in contact with as a result of serving under the Good $ense Ministry.

INTERVIEW OUTLINE FOR TEACHERS

Prior to the interview, review the candidate's application. The purpose of your interview with the teaching candidate is to determine whether he or she meets the qualification criteria. An additional purpose is to determine "soft" data—such as what the person is passionate or motivated about. Is he or she enthusiastic/excited about serving in a teaching capacity? Eager to learn? Is there evidence of a compassionate versus judgmental spirit? The following outline can be used to guide your interview.

1. Share an overview of the Good $ense Ministry and how it is a key ministry in the life and strategy of the church. Be an enthusiastic spokesperson for the ministry!

2. Ask:

   - Why are you interested in being a Good $ense teacher?
   - Describe your personal relationship with Jesus Christ. How is it growing?
   - How do you currently participate in the church?
   - What are your spiritual gifts?
   - Tell me about your financial life. Do you live on a budget? How do you make financial decisions?
   - Have you had any prior teaching experience?
   - Is there a special area/topic you would especially like to teach about?
   - Are you willing to do the necessary preparation to teach the Good $ense courses? This includes thoroughly reading the Leader's Guide, holding practice sessions with other teachers or core team members, reading other resources to deepen your understanding of Biblical Financial Principles, considering visiting another church to experience the course if practical.

3. Provide the candidate with a copy of Qualifications of a Good $ense Teacher (see page 112). Point out the Good $ense policy that no teacher may sell or profit from a product or service he or she can offer to an individual or family he or she is personally working with or have come in contact with as a result of his or her serving under the Good $ense Ministry.

4. Ask what questions the candidate has about the Good $ense Ministry.

5. Promote the Good $ense Ministry!

When the interview is complete, write your comments on the bottom of the Volunteer Application form (see page 154).

INTERVIEW OUTLINE FOR COUNSELORS

Prior to the interview, review the candidate's application. The purpose of your interview with the counseling candidate is to determine whether he or she meets the qualification criteria. An additional purpose is to determine "soft" data—such as what the person is passionate or motivated about. Why does the person desire to be a budget counselor? Is he or she enthusiastic/excited about serving in this capacity? Eager to learn? Is there evidence of a compassionate versus judgmental spirit? The following outline can be used to guide your interview.

1. Share an overview of the Good $ense Ministry and how it is a key ministry in the life and strategy of the church. (Be an enthusiastic spokesperson for the ministry!)

2. Ask:

   - Why are you interested in being a Good $ense counselor?
   - What personal or professional budget experience do you have?
   - Describe your personal relationship with Jesus Christ. How is it growing?
   - How do you currently participate in the church?
   - What are your spiritual gifts?
   - Tell me about your financial life. Do you live on a budget? How do you make financial decisions?
   - Are you willing to attend the Good $ense Counselor Training Workshop?

3. Review a copy of Qualifications of a Good $ense Counselor (see page 113), which they received with their application. Point out the Good $ense policy that no counselor may sell or profit from a product or service he or she can offer to an individual or family they are personally working with or have come in contact with as a result of serving under the Good $ense Ministry.

4. Mention that if the candidate is married, we welcome the participation of his or her spouse, even if she/he is not financially oriented. The spouse often adds a "soft" side to the counseling

relationship. It also provides the opportunity for a couple to minister together and gives greater flexibility in assigning single women or men to a counselor.

5. Ask what questions the candidate has about the ministry.

6. Promote the Good $ense Ministry!

When the interview is complete, write your comments on the bottom of the Volunteer Application form (see page 154).

APPENDIX

GOOD $ENSE BUDGET COURSE

CONTENTS*

Sample *Good $ense Budget Course* Publicity
Sample *Good $ense Budget Course* Registration Confirmation Letter
Good $ense Budget Course Checklist

*Note: Pre-work for the *Good $ense Budget Course* appears in the Forms section on pages 157–172.

SAMPLE *GOOD $ENSE BUDGET COURSE* PUBLICITY

The **Good $ense Ministry**
of First Community Church

presents

The Good $ense Budget Course

January 20, 2003
9:00 A.M. – 4:00 P.M.
(Box lunch provided.)

First Community Church

1234 Main Street
Windy City, IL 60010

Phone (123) 555-0000
Fax (123) 555-1000

E-mail: info@firstcommunitychurch.org
Web site: www.firstcommunitychurch.org

Good $ense Ministry
First Community Church
1234 Main Street
Windy City, IL 60010

Place Stamp Here

GOOD $ENSE MINISTRY

"For where your treasure is, there your heart will be also."—Matthew 6:21

Jesus taught that how we use our money is an indication of our values and priorities. For many of us, organizing our finances according to Biblical Financial Principles can be hindered by the pull of our materialistic culture, a lack of knowledge about wise financial practices, and the need for effective tools to implement them.

Would you like to discover the peace and contentment that come from managing your financial resources according to God's purposes and principles?

The *Good $ense Budget Course* is designed to help you do just that. In this hands-on course, you'll learn how to honor God in your finances by becoming a . . .

- ◆ **Diligent Earner**
- ◆ **Generous Giver**
- ◆ **Wise Saver**
- ◆ **Cautious Debtor**
- ◆ **Prudent Consumer**

WHAT WILL I LEARN?

You will learn what the Bible teaches about finances and how to combat cultural myths such as, "Debt is expected and unavoidable," "Things bring happiness," and "A little more money will solve all your problems."

During the course, you will develop a Spending Plan for the coming year. You will learn about and choose between three different record-keeping systems to help you stick to your plan. Most importantly, you will discover how being financially faithful can help you to become financially free!

Pre-work materials need to be completed prior to attending the course and will be given to you when you register. Spending an hour or two completing the pre-work will ensure you get the most benefit from the course. These materials are confidential and you will not be asked to share them with others.

You will leave the course with a Spending Plan in your hand, the knowledge in your head to implement it, and the motivation in your heart to follow through with it.

GOOD $ENSE BUDGET COURSE REGISTRATION

January 20, 2003
9:00 A.M. – 4:00 P.M.

Cost
The registration fee is $15 for individuals and $25 for couples. The fee includes the cost for materials and a box lunch for each participant.

Preparation
Please note that pre-work materials need to be completed prior to attending the course.

Registration Deadline
To register for the course, please complete the information below and return it along with your registration fee to the church office by January 13, 2003.

Name(s) _____

Street _____

City, State Zip code _____

Day Phone _____

Evening Phone _____

Cell Phone _____

Fax _____

E-mail _____

SAMPLE *GOOD $ENSE BUDGET COURSE* REGISTRATION CONFIRMATION LETTER

This letter should be given out at registration along with the *Good $ense Budget Course* Participant's Guide or pre-work packet.

Dear *Good $ense Budget Course* Participant:

We're glad you're registered for the *Good $ense Budget Course!* Regardless of one's financial situation, a budget, or Spending Plan, is the necessary and fundamental tool that enables you to control your money rather than having your money control you. Contrary to popular thought, it is not restrictive, but rather it is freedom-producing. We believe this course will prove the truth of that to you. Please note the information below.

Goal
The goal of the course is for you to develop and commit to a first-draft, biblically-based Spending Plan. We desire that you leave with your Spending Plan in hand, the knowledge in your head to implement it, and a commitment in your heart to follow through on it. Our commitment is to provide you with the principles, practical steps, and individual assistance (where necessary), to help make that happen.

Pre-work
The pre-work is important for the course to be as valuable and productive as possible. Please complete the pre-work BEFORE THE COURSE. Completion may take several hours, so we recommend you begin as soon as possible. The information you are asked to collect is confidential and no one else will see it. Throughout the course, you will use your pre-work information to establish your personal Spending Plan.

Supplies
In addition to your completed pre-work, please bring a couple pencils, an eraser, and your pocket calculator to the course.

Food
For your convenience, coffee and doughnuts will be available at 8:00 A.M. Drinks will be provided throughout the day, and lunch is provided as part of your registration fee.

Time
The workshop will begin at 9:00 A.M. sharp and end by 4:00 P.M.

Prayer
Please pray that this experience will be a valuable one for you and the others in attendance, and that we all grow in our understanding of Biblical Financial Principles and our ability to put them into practice.

Looking forward to seeing you there!

The Good $ense Ministry

GOOD $ENSE BUDGET COURSE CHECKLIST

As Far Out as Possible
- ❏ Set course dates
- ❏ Reserve room and equipment*
- ❏ Determine lunch arrangements (bring your own, catered, etc.)**

Eight Weeks Prior to Course
- ❏ Order *Good $ense Budget Course* Participant's Guides
- ❏ Prepare registration materials
- ❏ Prepare announcements/ advertising/ letters to send to membership

Six Weeks Prior to Course
- ❏ Put up posters in the church announcing the course
- ❏ Place the initial announcement in the church bulletin/weekly publication

Four Weeks Prior to Course
- ❏ Begin regular announcements in church bulletin/weekly publication
- ❏ Begin regular announcements or integration into messages during services
- ❏ Open registration and make Participant's Guides or pre-work available
- ❏ Confirm room reservation and arrangements
- ❏ Rehearse complete presentation

One Week Prior to Course
- ❏ Order food (snacks and lunches if applicable)
- ❏ Purchase supplies (extra pencils, calculators, name tags, etc.)

Day Before the Course

Registration Area
- ❏ Make sure registration materials and Participant's Guides are available for walk-in registrants

Equipment
- ❏ Put podium in place
- ❏ Set up and test sound system
- ❏ Make sure PowerPoint slide show is loaded and projector tested or overhead projector set up and overheads in order
- ❏ Make sure video equipment is set up, tested, and video loaded and cued

Room
- ❏ Make sure tables and chairs are set up
- ❏ Check lighting

Morning of Course
- ❏ Pray for God's blessing on the course
- ❏ Place any materials, announcements, or handouts on the tables
- ❏ Set out food and/or drinks
- ❏ Assign counselors to tables
- ❏ Do a final sound check
- ❏ Begin "Financial Quotes" PowerPoint presentation

Note: This serves as a guideline only. Actual times at your church may vary.
* Participants should have tables (preferably round) to work at.
** Lunch should not be off-site.

RECOMMENDED RESOURCES

Books

Randy Alcorn, *Money, Possessions and Eternity*. Tyndale House Publishers, 1989.

Excellent integration of biblical truths and practical ways to live them out. Very challenging. Highly recommended for all counselors.

Randy Alcorn, *The Treasure Principle*. Multhomah Press, 2001.

An in-depth study of the significance and joy of giving.

Ron Blue, *Master Your Money*. Thomas Nelson, 1997.

Nuts and bolts information and forms presented in a biblical context.

Larry Burkett, *The Word on Finances*. Moody Press, 1994.

Burkett has organized relevant Scriptures into this reference guide with more than seventy topics included under eight major headings. Each topic is preceded by a brief commentary. A helpful reference.

Larry Crabb, *Connecting*. W Publishing, 1997.

Crabb casts a vision that communities of ordinary Christians might better accomplish most of the good we now depend on mental health professionals to provide. While Good $ense counselors cannot replace mental health professionals, "connecting" with clients and helping them with their personal finances can accomplish much more than we often imagine. This is an excellent book from which to gain a deeper understanding of the potential impact of a counselor's role.

David Henderson, *Culture Shift*. Baker Books, 1998.

In part two entitled, "Who We Are: Consumers," Henderson gives a well-documented history and analysis of how our culture has "manufactured the consumer." Interesting and sobering reading.

Mary Hunt, *Mary Hunt's Debt-Proof Your Kids*. Broadman and Holman Publishers, 1998.

An excellent, hard-hitting book with lots of straight talk and good ideas for debt-proofing kids. Hunt also publishes the *Cheapskate Monthly* newsletter, which can be ordered by calling 800-550-3502.

Rollo May, *Art of Counseling*, Revised Edition. Amereon Press, 1989.

Good book on counseling techniques.

John Ortberg, Laurie Pederson, Judson Poling, *Giving: Unlocking the Heart of Good Stewardship*. Zondervan, 2000.

The questions at the end of each chapter of this small group study guide make it good material for group study and discussion.

Austin Pryor, *Sound Mind Investing*, Revised Edition. Victor Books, 2000.

Pryor does an excellent job of presenting thoroughly researched material on a complex topic in layperson's terms . . . and does it all from a clear Christian perspective. He also publishes a monthly newsletter and has a website that's well worth checking into: www.soundmindinvesting.com

David Ramsey, *Financial Peace*. Viking Press, 1992, 1997.

Practical advice on avoiding "stuffitis" and on learning how sacrifices now can produce long-term peace.

Juliet B. Schor, *The Overspent American*. HarperCollins, 1998.

Schor is a senior lecturer at Harvard and a professor at Tilburg University who has analyzed the crisis of the American consumer in a culture where "spending has become the ultimate social act." Not written from a Christian perspective but full of thought-provoking information.

Thomas J. Stanley, William D. Danko, *The Millionaire Next Door.* Longstreet Press, 1996.

This book reveals seven common factors characteristic of those who have accumulated wealth. These factors, as well as the identity of the millionaires, may surprise you.

Audio Tapes

The following audio tapes may be obtained by calling (800) 570-9812 or by logging on to www.willowcreek.com. Tapes used for seeker services at Willow Creek are prefaced with an M.

M0014	Bill Hybels	*Living Excellent Lives Financially*
M0003	Bill Hybels	*Tools for the New Millenium: The Palm Pilot*
M0004	Bill Hybels	*The Calculator and Managing Your Finances*
M0042	John Ortberg	*It All Goes Back in the Box*
C9516	John Ortberg	*What Jesus Really Taught about Greed*
M9402	Bill Hybels	*The Truth about Earthly Treasures*
C9122	Bill Hybels	*The Gift of Giving*
M9903	Bill Hybels	*The Financial Ten Commandments*
M9816 M9817 M9818	Bill Hybels	*What Money Can't Buy* (three-tape series)
M9949	Bill Hybels	*Truths that Transform, Part 9: Learn to be Content in All Circumstances*
DF9906	Bill Hybels/ Dick Towner	*Establishing Financial Good $ense*

Downloadable Message Transcripts and Drama Scripts

To provide you and/or your church with a solid basis for teaching biblical financial stewardship, message transcripts and drama scripts are available through the Willow Creek Asociation website. Suggested topics are listed on the next page.

To order or view these resources, go to:
www.willowcreek.com
- select "Service Builder"
- choose topic (suggested topics on the next page)
- choose type of media (message transcriopt or drama script)
- choose target audience
- select "Build Service"

This will take you to all media available under the topic you selected.
- select the desired message or drama by title
- add to your shopping cart

Once you have completed your transaction, you will be able to print out the transcript of the message and/or drama script you selected.

Topic: Money Management

Message Tapes

- All About Earning
- Debt—NO, Savings—YES
- Devoted to Each Other
- Faith and Finances
- The Gift of Giving
- Giving
- Giving to God's Work
- Gracious Generosity
- Leveraging Your Money for Eternity
- Living Excellent Lives, Part 3: Financially
- Making Change, Part 1: Credit Check
- Making Change, Part 2: Overdrawn
- Making Change, Part 3: A Balanced Account
- Mastering Your Mondy
- Money, Sex, and Power, Part 1: Who Owns What
- Money, Sex, and Power, Part 2: The Financial Ten Commandments
- Preparing a Freedom Plan
- Tools for the New Millenium, Part 3: Calculator—Managing You

Drama Scripts

- Catalog-itis
- Check It Out
- Check Mates
- Confessions of an Ad-aholic
- Lifestyles of the Obscured and Indebted
- Not Home
- The Offering
- Oh, What a Feeling!
- Rough Sale-ing
- The Financial Wizard

Topic: Contentment

Message Tapes
- Contentment
- It All Goes Back in the Box

Drama Scripts
- Early One Morning Just After the Dawn of History as We Know It
- Simple Gifts

Topic: Materialism/Greed

Message Tapes
- Living for More and Getting Less
- The Truth about Earthly Treasures
- Words to the Rich

Drama Scripts
- All I Want for Christmas
- The Box

Topic: Success

Message Tapes
- The Eighties
- Achievement's Shadow
- Bill Gates
- Defining Our Personal Aspirations
- Fifty and Reflecting
- Loving Mondays, Part 2: Optimizing Your Vocational Potential
- Madonna
- Michael Jordan
- The Middle Years
- Scruples
- Work as a Calling

Drama Scripts
- Driven
- The Legacy
- Lifetime Deal
- The Mirror Thought of It
- One Step Up, One Step Down

APPENDIX

FORMS

This section contains the following forms and documents to assist you in launching and leading your Good $ense Ministry.

- Client Profile
- Tips for Filling Out Your Client Profile
- Client Profile Analysis Chart
- Good $ense Budget Counseling Covenant
- Spending Record
- Spending Plan
- Debt Reduction Plan
- Client Progress Report
- Case Completion Report
- Client Counseling Evaluation Form
- Volunteer Application
- Core Team Commitment Form
- *Good $ense Budget Course* Pre-work

These forms are perforated so they can be removed, photocopied, and kept on file for use in your Good $ense Ministry. Electronic copies of these forms are also available on the *Good $ense Counselor Training Workshop* CD-ROM and/or the *Good $ense Budget Course* CD-ROM.

Client Profile

Good $ense Ministry

Number _____

Date Mailed _____

Date Received _____

Date Counselor Assigned _____

Name of Counselor _____

Counseling Completed _____

NAME_____ AGE _____

MARITAL STATUS _____

SPOUSE'S NAME _____

ADDRESS _____

CITY_____ ZIP _____

HOME PHONE (   ) _____

WORK PHONE (   ) _____

NATURE OF EMPLOYMENT:

    SELF_____

    SPOUSE _____

NAME(S)/AGE(S) OF CHILDREN _____

_____

_____

_____

WHAT I OWN

Checking Accounts _____

Savings Account _____

Other Savings _____

Insurance (cash value) _____

Retirement Funds _____

Home (market value) _____

Auto (age____ make_____) _____

Auto (age____ make_____) _____

Other Possessions (estimate) _____

Money Owed to Me _____

Other _____

Other _____

WHAT I OWE

	Total Owed	Min. Mo. Payment	Interest	Other	Total Owed	Min. Mo. Payment	Interest
Mortgage (current bal.)	$_____	_____	____%	_____	$_____	_____	____%
Home Equity Loan	_____	_____	____%	_____	_____	_____	____%
Credit Cards:	_____	_____	____%	_____	_____	_____	____%
_____	_____	_____	____%	_____	_____	_____	____%
_____	_____	_____	____%	_____	_____	_____	____%
_____	_____	_____	____%	_____	_____	_____	____%
_____	_____	_____	____%	_____	_____	_____	____%
Car Loans	_____	_____	____%	_____	_____	_____	____%
Education Loans	_____	_____	____%	_____	_____	_____	____%
Family/Friends	_____	_____	____%	_____	_____	_____	____%

WHAT I MAKE

Use take-home pay figures (the amount of the check):

Job #1 $_____ ☐ weekly ☐ every other week
                     ☐ monthly ☐ twice a month

My spouse gets a check for:

Job #1 $_____ ☐ weekly ☐ every other week
                     ☐ monthly ☐ twice a month

Job #2 $_____ ☐ weekly ☐ every other week
                     ☐ monthly ☐ twice a month

Job #2 $_____ ☐ weekly ☐ every other week
                     ☐ monthly ☐ twice a month

Other Income (explain)_____

Total Monthly Income_____

WHAT I SPEND

EARNINGS/INCOME PER MONTH
Salary #1 (net take-home) _____
Salary #2 (net take-home) _____
Other (less taxes) _____
TOTAL MONTHLY INCOME: _____

GIVING
   Church _____
   Other Contrib. _____
TOTAL GIVING _____

SAVINGS _____
TOTAL SAVINGS _____

DEBT
CREDIT CARDS
   Visa _____
   Master Card _____
   Discover _____
   Am. Express _____
   Gas Cards _____
   Dept. Stores _____
EDUCATION LOANS _____
OTHER LOANS:
   Bank Loans _____
   Credit Union _____
   Family/Friends _____
   Other _____
TOTAL DEBT _____

HOUSING
MORTGAGE/TAXES/RENT _____
MAINTENANCE/REPAIRS _____
UTILITIES:
   Electric _____
   Gas _____
   Water _____
   Trash _____
   Telephone/Internet _____
   Cable TV _____
OTHER _____
TOTAL HOUSING _____

AUTO/TRANSPORTATION
CAR PAYMTS./LICENSE _____
GAS/BUS/TRAIN/PKING. _____
OIL/LUBE/MAINT. _____
TOTAL AUTO _____

INSURANCE (paid by you)
AUTO _____
HOMEOWNERS _____
LIFE _____
MEDICAL/DENTAL _____
OTHER: _____
TOTAL INSURANCE _____

HOUSEHOLD/PERSONAL
GROCERIES _____
CLOTHES/DRYCLEANING _____
GIFTS _____
HOUSEHOLD ITEMS _____
PERSONAL
   Liquor/Tobacco _____
   Cosmetics _____
   Barber/Beauty _____
OTHER
   Books/Magazines _____
   Allowances _____
   Music Lessons _____
   Personal Technology _____
   Education _____
   Miscellaneous _____
TOTAL HOUSEHOLD _____

ENTERTAINMENT
GOING OUT:
   Meals _____
   Movies/Events _____
   Babysitting _____
TRAVEL (VAC./TRIPS) _____
OTHER:
   Fitness/Sports _____
   Hobbies _____
   Media Rental _____
   Other _____
TOTAL ENTERTAINMENT _____

PROFESSIONAL SERVICES
CHILD CARE _____
MED./DENTAL/PRESCRIP. _____
OTHER:
   Legal _____
   Counseling _____
   Union/Prof. Dues _____
   Other _____
TOTAL PROFESSIONAL _____

MISC. SMALL CASH EXPENSES _____

TOTAL EXPENSES _____

TOTAL MONTHLY INCOME	$_____
LESS TOTAL EXPENSES	$_____
INCOME OVER/(UNDER) EXPENSES	$_____

REQUEST

How can the Good $ense Ministry help you? _____
_____
_____
_____

What steps are you taking to improve your present situation?_____
_____
_____
_____
_____
_____
_____

Have you ever seen a financial planner/advisor? ❏ Yes ❏ No   If yes, who? _____
How were you helped? _____
_____
_____
_____

AGREEMENT

MY (OUR) AGREEMENT WITH _____

I (we) hereby make the commitment to actively participate with the Good $ense Ministry in seeking a resolution to the issues that brought me (us) to this place.

I (we) understand that Good $ense will attempt to assist me (us) in developing a plan, and that the consultant or volunteer agents do not make any representations or warranties with respect to the results of its services or its ability to help me (us) with my (our) credit/financial management.

I (we) understand that Good $ense is being offered to me (us) without charge or obligation, and that the people in Good $ense are volunteers who are donating their time to people requesting their assistance. Good $ense personnel have pledged to not benefit monetarily in any way as a result of their involvement in the ministry and are thereby prohibited from selling any services or products to persons who seek their counsel.

I (we) further agree to indemnify and hold harmless all volunteers of the Good $ense Ministry, the sponsor church and its employees, agents, counselors, officers, and directors from any claim, suit, action, demand or liability of any kind and any nature arising out of, or in any manner connected with, my (our) participation in Good $ense.

X _____   Date _____

X _____   Date _____

(If married, both spouses should sign.)

TIPS FOR FILLING OUT YOUR CLIENT PROFILE

The information on your Client Profile is confidential. Please fill it out as completely and accurately as possible. The information will be used by you and your counselor to develop a budget and debt retirement plan.

Please return the Client Profile as soon as possible.

WHAT I OWN

Fill in the blanks as requested. For "Other Possessions," simply estimate the market value of your major assets. If you had to sell everything, what would you be able to get?

WHAT I OWE

What liabilities do you have? To whom do you owe money and how much? What interest rate are you paying on each debt? Include the minimum monthly payment on each debt.

WHAT I MAKE

The income figures should be those which you *take home* after taxes and other deductions. Make a note of any deductions other than taxes (such as medical insurance, retirement, etc.). Where those items occur under expenses, enter an asterisk with the footnote "payroll deduction." If your income varies from month to month, use a conservative monthly average based on the last two or three years' earnings. Referring back to your income tax records could be helpful in that determination. Remember, you want to note after-tax, take-home income.

WHAT I SPEND

Gather as much information as you can to determine a *monthly average* for expenses in each category. Going through your check book register for the past year will probably be helpful. Be sure to include such items as auto insurance, property taxes, etc., that may not be paid on a monthly basis. If you've not kept records in the past, some of the categories may be difficult to estimate. Give it your best shot, recognizing that if you don't have records showing how much you're spending in a particular area, it's probably more than you think!

If what you are spending adds up to more than your take-home income, changes will need to be made. Your counselor will help clarify your options. Some changes may not be easy to make, but when done with a willing spirit, God will be pleased and will help! We look forward to working with you.

The Good $ense Ministry

Client: _____

Date: _____

Client Profile Analysis Chart

As you review the Client Profile, note positive things you can affirm and questions you want to ask. Place a check in the + or ? colums to indicate whether it is an affirmation or a question.

CHECKLIST	+	?	NOTES
FRONT COVER			
Is the client married? If so, the spouse should participate in the counseling meetings.			
How old is the client? This will give you an idea about future career income and of how adequate their savings are for college expenses and retirement, etc.			
What is the nature of the client's employment? If self-employed, there may be income stability issues and a question of whether they are current on their quarterly estimated tax payments.			
What are the names and ages of the client's children? This will help you understand the types and amount of their expenses as well as provide information that may be helpful in building rapport with your client.			
WHAT I OWN			
How much money is in the checking and savings accounts? This indicates whether your client has any buffer to work with.			
Are there any other savings listed for the client to draw on? The cash value of life insurance may be such a resource.			

CHECKLIST	+	?	NOTES
WHAT I OWN (continued)			
Has the client begun to save for retirement?			
What is the value of the home? How much money is owed on the home (from the "What I Owe" section)? This is a key part of their overall financial evaluation.			
Check the ages of the cars. If the cars are old, a savings plan for a new used car may be a top priority.			
What is the value of other possessions? If high, there may be an opportunity to sell some assets to jump-start debt repayment.			
WHAT I OWE			
Total all the consumer debts. Include all debts, *except* mortgage.			
WHAT I MAKE			
Verify the total monthly income figure. Note the frequency of paychecks. "Every other week" means that there are twenty-six paychecks per year. "Weekly" means fifty-two checks per year. Since we are interested in monthly income, you'll have to do the math to calculate the monthly income. Note also that these pay arrangements can create some cash flow complexities since paydays come on different dates each month.			

QUESTIONS	+	?	NOTES
WHAT I SPEND			
Is the client giving and saving anything?			
How do the consumer debt payments in this section compare to the minimum monthly payments listed in the "What I Owe" section?			
Based on the ages of the cars in the "What I Own" section, is a realistic amount listed for auto maintenance?			
Are there any missing items? Pay attention to the household/personal section. Clothes/dry cleaning, gifts, cosmetics, and barber/beauty are typically underestimated or left blank, yet just about everyone has these expenses.			
Total the monthly expenses and subtract from the monthly income to get an idea of cash flow.			
Check for any expenses in any of the categories that appear to be unusually high. Be prepared to learn why these expenses are high.			

QUESTIONS	+	?	NOTES
REQUEST			
Carefully read the answers to the open-ended questions. Look for clues about the client's attitude toward his/her situation and for action steps you can affirm.			
AGREEMENT			
If your clients are married, check whether they both signed the agreement. If not, ask about it at the first meeting.			

Needed for the first meeting:

GOOD $ENSE
BUDGET COUNSELING COVENANT

As a Good $ense client, you are asked to commit to the following:

1. A *significant effort* to develop better financial habits.

2. Regular *prayer* for learning and adopting new financial practices.

3. *Honesty* and openness—no financial surprises two months down the road.

4. An *honest effort* to act upon the counselor's guidance.

5. A consistent commitment of *time,* more at first but then tapering off gradually.

6. A willingness on your part to *be accountable* to the budget you and your counselor design for you.

As a counselor, I commit to you:

1. *Encouragement.*

2. Regular thoughts and *prayers* for you and your situation.

3. Respect for your *privacy.* All information you convey to me is kept *confidential.*

4. *Time* to meet with you.

5. *Training* seminars to sharpen my skills and knowledge.

6. My *skills* and expertise in budget counseling and the application of the Biblical Financial Principles to my own life.

7. *Ideas* to challenge you in your spiritual growth in the financial area of your life.

_____   _____
Client Signature   Counselor Signature

_____
Spouse Signature

_____   _____
Date   Date

BIBLICAL FINANCIAL PRINCIPLES

Steward's Mindset

God created everything. (Genesis 1:1)
God owns everything. (Psalms 24:1; 50:10, 12b)
We are trustees. (1 Corinthians 4:1-2)

Earning

Be diligent. (Colossians 3:23)
Be purposeful. (Colossians 3:23; 1 Timothy 5:8)
Be grateful. (Deuteronomy 8:18)

Giving

Giving is a key to a satisfied and fulfilled life. We are to give:

As a response to God's goodness. (James 1:17)
To focus on God as our source of security. (Matthew 6:19-20a; 23b-33)
To achieve economic justice.
To bless others. (Genesis 12:2-3)
To break the hold of money.

Saving

It is wise to save. (Proverbs 6:8; 21:20)
It is sinful to hoard. (Luke 12:16-21)

Debt

Repay debt. (Psalm 37:21)
Avoid debt. (Proverbs 22:7)

Spending

Beware of idols. (Deuteronomy 5:8; Romans 1:25)
Guard against greed. (Luke 12:15)
Be content. (Philippians 4:12)

Month _____

Spending Record

	Daily Variable Expenses									
	Transportation				Household				Professional Services	Entertainment	
	Gas, etc.	Maint/ Repair	Groceries	Clothes	Gifts	Household Items	Personal	Other		Going Out	Travel	Other
(1) Spending Plan												
1												
2												
3												
4												
5												
6												
7												
8												
9												
10												
11												
12												
13												
14												
15												
16												
17												
18												
19												
20												
21												
22												
23												
24												
25												
26												
27												
28												
29												
30												
31												
(2) Total												
(3) (Over)/Under												
(4) Last Month YTD												
(5) Total Year–to–Date												

- Use this page to record expenses that tend to be daily, variable expenses—often the hardest to control.
- Keep receipts throughout the day and record them at the end of the day.
- Total each category at the end of the month (line 2) and compare to the Spending Plan (line 1). Subtracting line 2 from line 1 gives you an (over) or under the budget figure for that month (line 3).
- To verify that you have made each day's entry, cross out the number at the bottom of the page that corresponds to that day's date.
- Optional: If you wish to monitor your progress as you go through the year, you can keep cumulative totals in lines 4 and 5.

Spending Record

Month _____

Monthly Regular Expenses
(generally paid by check once a month)

	Giving		Savings	Debt				Housing				Auto	Insurance		Misc. Cash Exp.
	Church	Other		Credit Cards	Educ.	Other	Mort./Rent	Maint.	Util.	Other		Pmts.	Auto/Home	Life/Med.	
(1) Spending Plan															
(2) Total															
(3) (Over)/Under															
(4) Last Mo. YTD															
(5) This Mo. YTD															

- This page allows you to record major monthly expenses for which you typically write just one or two checks per month.
- Entries can be recorded as the checks are written (preferably) or by referring back to the check ledger at a convenient time.
- Total each category at the end of the month (line 2) and compare to the Spending Plan (line 1). Subtracting line 2 from line 1 gives you an (over) or under the budget figure for that month (line 3).
- Use the "Monthly Assessment" section to reflect on the future actions that will be helpful in staying on course.

Monthly Assessment

Area	(Over)/Under	Reason	Future Action

Areas of Victory _____

Areas to Watch _____

SPENDING PLAN

EARNINGS/INCOME PER MONTH	TOTALS
Salary #1 (net take-home)	_____
Salary #2 (net take-home)	_____
Other (less taxes)	_____
TOTAL MONTHLY INCOME	$_____

% GUIDE

1. GIVING $_____
- Church _____
- OTHER CONTRIBUTIONS _____

2. SAVING   5–10% $_____
- EMERGENCY _____
- REPLACEMENT _____
- LONG TERM _____

3. DEBT   0–10% $_____
- CREDIT CARDS:
  - VISA _____
  - Master Card _____
  - Discover _____
  - American Express _____
  - Gas Cards _____
  - Department Stores _____
- EDUCATION LOANS _____
- OTHER LOANS:
  - Bank Loans _____
  - Credit Union _____
  - Family/Friends _____
  - OTHER _____

4. HOUSING   25–38% $_____
- MORTGAGE/TAXES/RENT _____
- MAINTENANCE/REPAIRS _____
- UTILITIES:
  - Electric _____
  - Gas _____
  - Water _____
  - Trash _____
  - Telephone/Internet _____
  - Cable TV _____
- OTHER _____

5. AUTO/TRANSP.   12–15% $_____
- CAR PAYMENTS/LICENSE _____
- GAS & BUS/TRAIN/PARKING _____
- OIL/LUBE/MAINTENANCE _____

* This is a % of total monthly income. These are guidelines only and may be different for individual situations. However, there should be good rationale for a significant variance.

6. INSURANCE (Paid by you)   5% $_____
- AUTO _____
- HOMEOWNERS _____
- LIFE _____
- MEDICAL/DENTAL _____
- Other _____

7. HOUSEHOLD/PERSONAL   15–25% $_____
- GROCERIES _____
- CLOTHES/DRY CLEANING _____
- GIFTS _____
- HOUSEHOLD ITEMS _____
- PERSONAL:
  - Liquor/Tobacco _____
  - Cosmetics _____
  - Barber/Beauty _____
- OTHER:
  - Books/Magazines _____
  - Allowances _____
  - Music Lessons _____
  - Personal Technology _____
  - Education _____
  - Miscellaneous _____

8. ENTERTAINMENT   5–10% $_____
- GOING OUT:
  - Meals _____
  - Movies/Events _____
  - Baby-sitting _____
- TRAVEL (VACATION/TRIPS) _____
- OTHER:
  - Fitness/Sports _____
  - Hobbies _____
  - Media Rental _____
  - OTHER _____

9. PROF. SERVICES   5–15% $_____
- CHILD CARE _____
- MEDICAL/DENTAL/PRESC. _____
- OTHER
  - Legal _____
  - Counseling _____
  - Professional Dues _____

10. MISC. SMALL CASH EXPENDITURES   2–3% $_____

TOTAL EXPENSES $_____

TOTAL MONTHLY INCOME	$_____
LESS TOTAL EXPENSES	$_____
INCOME OVER/(UNDER) EXPENSES	$_____

Debt Reduction Plan

Item	Amount Owed	Interest	Minimum Monthly Payment	Additional Payment $_____	Payment Plan and Pay-off Dates					
Total										

- The first and second columns list to whom the debt is owed and the amount owed. Debts are listed in the order of lowest to highest amount.
- The third and fourth columns list the interest rate and the minimum monthly payment for each debt.
- The fifth column indicates the amount of additional payment above the minimum that can be made and adds that amount to the minimum payment for the first (smallest) debt listed.
- The remaining columns show how, as each debt is paid, the payment for it is rolled down to the next debt. Pay-off dates can be calculated in advance or simply recorded as they are achieved.

Client Progress Report
Good $ense Ministry

Counselor _____   **Case No.** _____

Client _____

Instructions: This report serves as a summarized record of meetings with your client. Include the results of previous action items, observations about your client's behavior and attitudes, thoughts on your client's progress, and action items assigned for the next meeting. At the completion of this case, all progress reports should be forwarded to the ministry office.

Meeting Date: _____   Next Meeting Date: _____

Time: _____   Time: _____

Results of previous action items:
_____
_____
_____

Observations about the client's behavior and attitudes:
_____
_____
_____
_____
_____
_____

Thoughts on the client's progress:
_____
_____
_____
_____
_____
_____

Action items assigned for the next meeting:
_____
_____
_____
_____
_____

Observations about the client's spiritual condition:
_____
_____
_____
_____

CASE COMPLETION REPORT
Good $ense Ministry

Instructions: At the completion of a case, this form should be forwarded with the Client Progress Reports to the Good $ense administrator.

Date _____   **Client Name** _____

Last date of contact _____   **Counselor** _____

How terminated: ❏ In person   ❏ By telephone   ❏ No contact

Who decided: ❏ Mutual   ❏ Counselor   ❏ Client

In view of counselor:
Original problem that brought about referral : _____
_____

Is this problem now: ❏ Resolved   ❏ Improved   ❏ Unchanged   ❏ Worse

Additional problems worked on: Is each problem:
_____   ❏ Resolved   ❏ Improved   ❏ Unchanged   ❏ Worse
_____   ❏ Resolved   ❏ Improved   ❏ Unchanged   ❏ Worse

NOTE: Upon completion of a case, successful or unsuccessful, a goal is to have the client connected somewhere within the church—a ministry that can further help them or a small group that can help them grow, etc. Please indicate the results of your efforts in that regard: Client ❏ Is ❏ Is NOT connected elsewhere. Explain:
_____
_____

Counseling Results:
Success is judged by the following criteria: 1) the client is embracing the Biblical Financial Principles and making decisions based upon these principles; 2) the client has a Spending Plan in place and has been following it for at least three months; 3) the client has a Debt Reduction Plan in place and has been following it for at least three months; 4) the client has met his/her goals.

❏ Successful   ❏ Partial   ❏ Unsuccessful
(met all criteria)   (met some criteria)   (met no criteria)

Comments:
_____
_____
_____
_____

Is there something about this case that could help and/or encourage other counselors or clients? If so, what?
_____
_____
_____
_____

CLIENT COUNSELING EVALUATION FORM

Good $ense Ministry

You recently met with _____, a counselor in the Good $ense Ministry. We hope your time together was helpful to you both spiritually and financially. We are always interested in improving our services, and your candid response to the following questions will help us do that. Your comments are confidential. Thanks for taking a moment to give us your feedback.

What was your primary reason for seeking counsel?

_____
_____

Was that reason addressed? Do you feel the counsel you received helped to resolve that issue?

_____
_____

Were Biblical Financial Principles used as a basis of the counsel? Please describe:

_____
_____

Did you find your counselor to be: Very   Moderately   Not at all
    Respectful and sensitive   ❑   ❑   ❑
    Knowledgeable   ❑   ❑   ❑
    Helpful   ❑   ❑   ❑

Our ministry policy states, "No counselor may sell or profit from a product or service they can offer to an individual or family they are personally working with or have come in contact with as a result of serving in the Good $ense counseling ministry." Was this ever an issue with your counselor?

_____
_____

Do you have any recommendations for how we might improve the ministry?

_____
_____

Additional comments:

_____
_____
_____

GOOD $ENSE MINISTRY

Volunteer Application

Name _____

Address _____   **Birth date** _____

_____   **Work phone** _____

Home phone _____   **Cell phone** _____

Fax _____   **E-mail** _____

Married _____   **Single** _____

Name of spouse and/or children _____

_____

Position for which you are applying (circle one):

   Core Team Member   Teacher   Counselor   Group Leader   Administrator   Other _____

Briefly describe your spiritual journey and how you came to know Jesus Christ.

_____

_____

Are you a member of the church? Yes ___ No ___

When did you start regularly attending the church? _____

Are you involved in other ministries? Yes ___ No ___

If yes, please briefly state which one(s) and the nature of your involvement.

_____

_____

Is there someone at the church who knows you well and could be a reference on your behalf? Please list their name and phone number:

_____

Do you know your spiritual gifts? Yes ___ No ___

If yes, what do you understand your spiritual gifts to be?

1. _____   2. _____   3. _____

Which, if any, Good $ense courses have you attended?

_____

Place of employment and nature of responsibilities:

Organization: _____

Responsibilities: _____

Would you stand to benefit financially or professionally from your association with this ministry?

Yes ____   No ____   If yes, how?

_____
_____

Do you feel you are modeling principles of good stewardship in your personal finances?

Yes ____   No ____

Please explain: _____
_____

What attracted you to serving in the Good $ense Ministry?

_____
_____
_____

What strengths/weaknesses do you believe you would bring to the ministry?

_____
_____
_____

APPLICANT, PLEASE DO NOT WRITE BELOW THIS LINE

Interviewer's comments and recommendation: _____

_____
_____
_____
_____
_____

For counselor candidates only:
   Candidate   Was___   Was not___   notified of the next *Good $ense Counselor Training Workshop*
               Was___   Was not___   given the Participant's Guide and Manual for the *Good $ense Counselor Training Workshop.*

_____
Interviewer's Signature

GOOD $ENSE
CORE TEAM COMMITMENT FORM

As a member of the core team, I commit to the following:

1. To faithfully attend core team member meetings, including training courses or visits to other ministries.

2. To diligently study with other core team members to more fully understand the Biblical Financial Principles.

3. To honor Biblical Financial Principles in my life.

4. To work as a team member to develop the proposal for a Good $ense Ministry and to provide ongoing leadership to the ministry.

_____
Signature

_____
Date

PRE-WORK FOR

THE GOOD $ENSE BUDGET COURSE

IMPORTANT

Please read and complete all pre-work prior to attending the course.

Dear Good $ense Budget Course Participant,

We're glad you're registered for the *Good $ense Budget Course*! Regardless of your financial situation, a budget—what we call a "Spending Plan"—is the necessary and fundamental tool that enables you to control your money rather than having your money control you. Contrary to popular thought, a Spending Plan is not restrictive; rather, it is freeing. We believe the *Good $ense Budget Course* will prove this truth to you.

Course Goal

The goal of the *Good $ense Budget Course* is for you to commit to and begin developing a biblically-based Spending Plan. By the end of the course, you will have a Spending Plan in your hand, the knowledge in your head to implement it, and a commitment in your heart to follow through on it. The commitment of the Good $ense Ministry is to provide you with the principles, practical steps, and individual assistance to help make that happen.

Pre-work

In order for the course to be as valuable and productive as possible, it is very important to complete the pre-work prior to attending the course. Completing the forms may take several hours so it is advisable to begin as soon as your receive these materials. The information you are asked to collect is confidential and no one else will see it. Throughout the course, you will use your pre-work information to establish your personal Spending Plan.

Supplies

In addition to your completed pre-work, please bring to the course two or three pencils, an eraser, and a pocket calculator.

Prayer

Pray that this experience will be a valuable one for you and the others in attendance, and that we will all grow in our understanding of Biblical Financial Principles and our ability to put them into practice.

Looking forward to seeing you there!

The Good $ense Ministry

PRE-WORK INSTRUCTIONS

Six forms are included in the pre-work to help you prepare for the *Good $ense Budget Course*. Please allow plenty of time prior to attending the course to gather the information and to complete each form. Instructions to help you complete each form are listed below.

Goals to Achieve this Year
Make it a priority to reflect on your financial goals. If you are married, make time to discuss financial goals with your spouse. These goals will become the basis for shaping your Spending Plan, and they will provide motivation for following through on your decisions in the months ahead.

What I Owe
As you fill out the second column (Amount) of this section, use the total balance due on each item.

What I Own
These sections are optional, but we encourage you to fill them out so you can calculate a simplified version of your "net worth." Consider that the value of things you own should be the amount you would expect to get if you sold the items.

Gift List
Here's an often overlooked or underestimated part of spending. Write the names of individuals you will be purchasing gifts for in the coming year. Remember to include cards, postage at Christmas, parties, etc. You may wish to include some money for as yet unannounced weddings, etc.

What I Spend
Gather as much information as you can to determine a monthly average for expenses in each category. Going through your checkbook and your credit card bills for the past year will probably be helpful. Be sure to include periodic expense items such as auto insurance, taxes, etc., that may not be paid on a monthly basis. If you have not kept records in the past, some of the categories may be difficult to estimate. Give it your best

shot, recognizing that if you don't have records showing how much you're spending in a particular area, the amount is probably more than you think it is!

The Income figures at the top of the page should be your take-home pay after taxes and other deductions. Make a note of any deductions (such as medical insurance, retirement, etc.). Where those items occur under expenses, enter the notation "payroll deduction." If your income varies from month to month, use a conservative monthly estimate based on the last two or three years' earnings. Referring back to your income tax records could be helpful in making this determination. Remember, you are looking for after-tax, take-home income.

Money Motivation Quiz

This is an optional exercise that will provide insightful information on your behavior regarding money. If you are married, two copies of the quiz are provided so you and your spouse can both take the quiz. Answers are included on the back of the quiz. No fair peeking before you answer the questions!

GOALS TO ACHIEVE THIS YEAR

Please allow adequate time to give serious consideration to your goals. Carefully considered, realistic goals—that flow out of what's really important to you—are powerful motivators. That motivation will be very helpful to you in following through on the steps necessary to achieve your goals.

OVERALL GOAL

My overall goal in attending this course is:

_____

_____

SPECIFIC GOALS TO ACHIEVE

Check the appropriate boxes and write in any details on the lines to the right of each item.

- ❑ Pay off debt: _____
- ❑ Save for a major purchase (home, car, other): _____
- ❑ Save for a dream vacation: _____
- ❑ Save for emergencies: _____
- ❑ Save to replace items that may wear out (major appliances, home repairs, car): _____
- ❑ Save for college expenses: _____
- ❑ Save for retirement: _____
- ❑ Increase my giving to the church: _____
- ❑ Increase other giving: _____
- ❑ Other: _____
- ❑ Other: _____
- ❑ Other: _____

PRE-WORK

What I Owe			
I Owe (liabilities)	Amount	Minimum Monthly Payment	Interest Percentage
Mortgage (current balance)			
Home Equity Loans			
Credit Cards			
Car Loans			
Education Loans			
Family/Friends			
Other			
Total of All I Owe			

What I Own (optional)	
I Own (assets)	Amount
Checking Account	
Savings Account	
Other Savings	
Insurance (cash value)	
Retirement	
Home (market value)	
Auto (market value)	
Second Auto (market value)	
Other Possessions (estimate)	
Money Owed to Me	
Other	
Other	
Total of All I Own	

Net Worth (optional)
(Total of All I Own – Total of All I owe = Net Worth (in earthly terms, not God's!)*

_____ – _____ = _____

*Never confuse your self-worth with your net worth. In God's eyes each one of us is of infinite worth.

PRE-WORK

P-9

GIFT LIST

List the names of those you for whom you buy gifts and the amounts you typically spend on each occasion.*

Name	Birthday	Christmas	Anniversary	Other
1.				
2.				
3.				
4.				
5.				
6.				
7.				
8.				
9.				
10.				
11.				
12.				
13.				
14.				
15.				
16.				
17.				
18.				
19.				
20.				
Total				

GRAND TOTAL $_____   MONTHLY AVERAGE (Total ÷ 12) = $_____
(of all columns)

*You may wish to also include the cost of holiday decorations, entertaining, etc.

SPENDING PLAN

EARNINGS/INCOME PER MONTH	TOTALS
Salary #1 (net take-home)	_____
Salary #2 (net take-home)	_____
Other (less taxes)	_____
TOTAL MONTHLY INCOME	$_____

% GUIDE

1. GIVING $_____
- Church _____
- OTHER CONTRIBUTIONS _____

2. SAVING 5–10% $_____
- EMERGENCY _____
- REPLACEMENT _____
- LONG TERM _____

3. DEBT 0–10% $_____
- CREDIT CARDS:
  - VISA _____
  - Master Card _____
  - Discover _____
  - American Express _____
  - Gas Cards _____
  - Department Stores _____
- EDUCATION LOANS _____
- OTHER LOANS:
  - Bank Loans _____
  - Credit Union _____
  - Family/Friends _____
  - OTHER _____

4. HOUSING 25–38% $_____
- MORTGAGE/TAXES/RENT _____
- MAINTENANCE/REPAIRS _____
- UTILITIES:
  - Electric _____
  - Gas _____
  - Water _____
  - Trash _____
  - Telephone/Internet _____
  - Cable TV _____
  - OTHER _____

5. AUTO/TRANSP. 12–15% $_____
- CAR PAYMENTS/LICENSE _____
- GAS & BUS/TRAIN/PARKING _____
- OIL/LUBE/MAINTENANCE _____

* This is a % of total monthly income. These are guidelines only and may be different for individual situations. However, there should be good rationale for a significant variance.

6. INSURANCE (Paid by you) 5% $_____
- AUTO _____
- HOMEOWNERS _____
- LIFE _____
- MEDICAL/DENTAL _____
- Other _____

7. HOUSEHOLD/PERSONAL 15–25% $_____
- GROCERIES _____
- CLOTHES/DRY CLEANING _____
- GIFTS _____
- HOUSEHOLD ITEMS _____
- PERSONAL:
  - Liquor/Tobacco _____
  - Cosmetics _____
  - Barber/Beauty _____
- OTHER:
  - Books/Magazines _____
  - Allowances _____
  - Music Lessons _____
  - Personal Technology _____
  - Education _____
  - Miscellaneous _____

8. ENTERTAINMENT 5–10% $_____
- GOING OUT:
  - Meals _____
  - Movies/Events _____
  - Baby-sitting _____
- TRAVEL (VACATION/TRIPS) _____
- OTHER:
  - Fitness/Sports _____
  - Hobbies _____
  - Media Rental _____
  - OTHER _____

9. PROF. SERVICES 5–15% $_____
- CHILD CARE _____
- MEDICAL/DENTAL/PRESC. _____
- OTHER
  - Legal _____
  - Counseling _____
  - Professional Dues _____

10. MISC. SMALL CASH EXPENDITURES 2–3% $_____

TOTAL EXPENSES $_____

TOTAL MONTHLY INCOME	$_____
LESS TOTAL EXPENSES	$_____
INCOME OVER/(UNDER) EXPENSES	$_____

MONEY MOTIVATION QUIZ

Directions
For each of the fourteen questions below, circle the letter that best describes your response.

1. Money is important because it allows me to . . .
   a. Do what I want to do.
   b. Feel secure.
   c. Get ahead in life.
   d. Buy things for others.

2. I feel that money . . .
   a. Frees up my time.
   b. Can solve my problems.
   c. Is a means to an end.
   d. Helps make relationships smoother.

3. When it comes to saving money, I . . .
   a. Don't have a plan and rarely save.
   b. Have a plan and stick to it.
   c. Don't have a plan but manage to save anyway.
   d. Don't make enough money to save.

4. If someone asks about my personal finances, I . . .
   a. Feel defensive.
   b. Realize I need more education and information.
   c. Feel comfortable and competent.
   d. Would rather talk about something else.

5. When I make a major purchase, I . . .
   a. Go with what my intuition tells me.
   b. Research a great deal before buying.
   c. Feel I'm in charge-it's my/our money.
   d. Ask friends/family first.

6. If I have money left over at the end of the month, I . . .
   a. Go out and have a good time.
   b. Put the money into savings.
   c. Look for a good investment.
   d. Buy a gift for someone.

7. If I discover I paid more for something than a friend did I . . .
   a. Couldn't care less.
   b. Feel it's okay because I also find bargains at times.
   c. Assume they spent more time shopping, and time is money.
   d. Feel upset and angry at myself.

8. When paying bills, I . . .
   a. Put it off and sometimes forget.
   b. Pay them when due, but no sooner.
   c. Pay when I get to it, but don't want to be hassled.
   d. Worry that my credit will suffer if I miss a payment.

9. When it comes to borrowing money I . . .
   a. Simply won't-don't like to feel indebted.
   b. Only borrow as a last resort.
   c. Tend to borrow from banks or other business sources.
   d. Ask friends and family because they know I'll pay.

10. When eating out with friends I prefer to . . .
    a. Divide the bill proportionately.
    b. Ask for separate checks.
    c. Charge the bill to my bankcard and have others pay me.
    d. Pay the entire bill because I like to treat my friends.

11. When it comes to tipping I . . .
    a. Sometimes do and sometimes don't.
    b. Just call me Scrooge.
    c. Resent it, but always tip the right amount.
    d. Tip generously because I like to be well thought of.

12. If I suddenly came into a lot of money, I . . .
    a. Wouldn't have to work.
    b. Wouldn't have to worry about the future.
    c. Could really build up my business.
    d. Would spend a lot on family and friends and enjoy time with them more.

13. When indecisive about a purchase I often tell myself . . .
    a. It's only money.
    b. It's a bargain.
    c. It's a good investment.
    d. He/she will love it.

14. In our family . . .
    a. I do/will handle all the money and pay all the bills.
    b. My partner does/will take care of the finances.
    c. I do/will pay my bills and my partner will do the same.
    d. We do/will sit down together to pay bills.

15. **Bonus question:** Describe how money was handled in your family of origin. Who managed the family budget? Was that person a spender or a saver? Which are you?

Score: Tally your answers to questions one through fourteen by the letter of your answer:

a. _____ c. _____
b. _____ d. _____

To understand your results, see the explanation on the back of this page.

UNDERSTANDING THE RESULTS OF YOUR MONEY MOTIVATION QUIZ

Money means different things to different people based on a variety of factors such as temperament and life experiences. Often the meaning of money and the way it motivates us is subtle and something we are not always aware of.

This simple quiz is designed to give you an indication of how strongly you are influenced by the following money motivations: Freedom, Security, Power, and Love. None are inherently good or bad, although each certainly has its dark side.

The key to your money motivation is reflected in the relative number of a, b, c, or d answers.

"A" answers indicate that money relates to **Freedom**. To you money means having the freedom to do what you like.

"B" answers indicate that money relates to **Security**. You need to feel safe and secure and you desire the stability and protection that money supposedly provides.

"C" answers indicate that money relates to **Power**. Personal success and control are important to you, and you appreciate the power money sometimes provides.

"D" answers indicate that money relates to **Love**. You like to use money to express love and build relationships.

One of the keys to managing money wisely is to understand our relationship to it. We hope this exercise gives you some helpful insights. You may wish to share your scores with your spouse or a friend and discuss whether their perceptions of your money motivations are consistent with your scores.

NOTES

NOTES

NOTES

NOTES

NOTES

NOTES

NOTES

NOTES

WILLOW CREEK ASSOCIATION

Vision, **Training,** **Resources**

for Prevailing Churches

This resource was created to serve you and to help you in building a local church that prevails!

Since 1992, the Willow Creek Association (WCA) has been linking like-minded, action-oriented churches with each other and with strategic vision, training, and resources. Now a worldwide network of over 7,000 churches from more than ninety denominations, the WCA works to equip Member Churches and others with the tools needed to build prevailing churches. Our desire is to inspire, equip, and encourage Christian leaders to build biblically functioning "Acts 2" churches that reach increasing numbers of unchurched people, not just with innovations from Willow Creek Community Church in South Barrington, Illinois, but from any church in the world that has experienced God-given breakthroughs.

Willow Creek Conferences

Each year, thousands of local church leaders, staff and volunteers—from WCA Member Churches and others—attend one of our conferences or training events. Conferences offered on the Willow Creek campus in South Barrington, Illinois, include:

- Prevailing Church Conference—Offered twice a year, it is the foundational, overarching, training conference for staff and volunteers working to build a prevailing local church.
- Select ministry workshops—A wide variety of strategic, day-long workshops covering seven topic areas that represent key characteristics of a prevailing church; offered multiple times throughout the year.
- Promiseland Conference—Children's ministries; infant through fifth grade.
- Student Ministries Conference—Junior and senior high ministries.
- Arts Conference—Vision and training for Christian artists using their gifts in the ministries of local churches.
- Leadership Summit—Envisioning and equipping Christians with leadership gifts and responsibilities; broadcast live via satellite to scores of cities across North America.
- Contagious Evangelism Conference—Encouragement and training for churches and church leaders who want to be strategic in reaching lost people for Christ.
- Small Groups Conference—Exploring how developing a church of small groups can play a vital role in developing authentic Christian community that leads to spiritual transformation.

To find out more about WCA conferences, visit our website at www.willowcreek.com.

Regional Conferences and Training Events

Each year the WCA team leads a variety of topical conferences and training events in select cities across the United States. Ministry and topic topic areas include leadership, next-generation ministries, small groups, arts and worship, evangelism, spiritual gifts, financial stewardship, and spiritual formation. These events make quality training more accessible and affordable to larger groups of staff and volunteers.

To find out more about upcoming events in your area, visit our website at www.willowcreek.com.

Willow Creek Resources®

Churches can look to Willow Creek Resources® for a trusted channel of ministry tools in areas of leadership, evangelism, spiritual gifts, small groups, drama, contemporary music, financial stewardship, spiritual transformation, and more. For ordering information, call (800) 570-9812 or visit our website at www.willowcreek.com.

WCA Membership

Membership in the Willow Creek Association as well as attendance at WCA Conferences is for churches, ministries, and leaders who hold to an historic, orthodox understanding of biblical Christianity. The annual church membership fee of $249 provides substantial discounts for your entire team on all conferences and Willow Creek Resources, networking opportunities with other outreach-oriented churches, a bimonthly newsletter, a subscription to the Defining Moments monthly audio journal for leaders, and more.

To find out more about WCA membership, visit our website at www.willowcreek.com.

WillowNet   www.willowcreek.com

This Internet resource service provides access to hundreds of Willow Creek messages, drama scripts, songs, videos, and multimedia ideas. The system allows you to sort through these elements and download them for a fee.

Our website also provides detailed information on the Willow Creek Association, Willow Creek Community Church, WCA membership, conferences, training events, resources, and more.

WillowCharts.com   www.WillowCharts.com

Designed for local church worship leaders and musicians, WillowCharts.com provides online access to hundreds of music charts and chart components, including choir, orchestral, and horn sections, as well as rehearsal tracks and video streaming of Willow Creek Community Church performances.

The NET http://studentministry.willowcreek.com

The NET is an online training and resource center designed by and for student ministry leaders. It provides an inside look at the structure, vision, and mission of prevailing student ministries from around the world. The NET gives leaders access to complete programming elements, including message outlines, dramas, small group questions, and more. An indispensable resource and networking tool for prevailing student ministry leaders!

Contact the Willow Creek Association

If you have comments or questions, or would like to find out more about WCA events or resources, please contact us:

Willow Creek Association
P.O. Box 3188
Barrington, IL 60011-3188
Phone: (800) 570-9812 or (847) 765-0070
Fax (888) 922-0035 or (847) 765-5046
Web: www.willowcreek.com

Resources You've Been Waiting For . . .
To Build the Church You've Been Dreaming About

Willow Creek Resources

What do you dream about for your church?

At the Willow Creek Association we have a dream for the church . . . one that envisions the local church—your church—as the focal point for individual and community transformation.

We want to partner with you to make this happen. We believe when authentic, life-changing resources become an integral part of everyday life at your church—and when they become an extension of how your ministries function—transformation is inevitable.

It then becomes normal for people to:
- identify their personal style of evangelism and use it to bring their unchurched friends to Christ
- grow in their ability to experience God's presence with them in each moment of the day
- feel a deep sense of community with others
- discover their spiritual gifts and put them to use in ministry
- use their resources in ways that honor God and care for others

If this is the kind of church you're dreaming about, keep reading. The following pages highlight just a few of the many Willow Creek Resources available to help you. Together, we can build a local church that transforms lives and transfigures communities. We can build a church that *prevails*.

BESTSELLING WILLOW CREEK RESOURCES

Everything You Need to Launch and Lead a Bi[...]

Good $ense

Transformational Stewardship for Today's Church

DICK TOWNER
with contributions from the Good $ense Ministry team of Willow Creek Community Church

GRACE. JOY. FREEDOM.
Are these the first words that come to mind when you think of stewardship? They could be! Grace, joy, and freedom are words people most often use to describe Good $ense—a field-tested, proven resource for changing hearts and lives in the area of finances.

There is a tremendous need for churches to educate and assist people with managing their resources in God-honoring ways. Implementing a Good $ense Ministry in your church does that. It can relieve the crushing stress and anxiety caused by consumer debt, restore marriages torn by conflict over money, and heal the wounded self-esteem and shattered confidence resulting from poor financial decisions.

Most significantly, a Good $ense Ministry can be used by God to remove stumbling blocks to spiritual growth. This is *transformational stewardship*. The result is a congregation whose finances—and lives—are characterized by grace, joy, and freedom.

Complete Kit	0744137241
Casting a Vision for Good $ense video	0744137268
Implementation Guide	074413725X
Budget Course Leader's Guide	0744137276
Budget Course Participant's Guide	0744137284
Budget Course Video	0744137292
Budget Course PowerPoint CD-ROM	0744137306
Counselor Training Workshop Leader's Guide	0744137314
Counselor Training Workshop Participant's Guide	0744137322
Counselor Training Workshop Video	0744137330
Counselor Training Workshop PowerPoint CD-ROM	0744137349

cal Stewardship Ministry that Transforms Lives

Based on over sixteen years of ministry at Willow Creek Community Church, Good $ense includes resources designed to train and equip: church leaders, volunteer counselors, and everyone in your church.

Envision Church Leaders and Implement the Ministry

Good $ense Implementation Guide
Casting a Vision for Good $ense Video

FOR: Senior church leaders.

PURPOSE: To envision and equip leaders to launch and lead a year-round stewardship ministry.

CONTENTS: The Implementation Guide provides a roadmap for implementing a Good $ense Ministry as well as the practical tools to do so. The video provides an inspiring tool to help leaders cast vision for a Good $ense Ministry.

Equip Volunteer Counselors

Good $ense Counselor Training Workshop

FOR: Volunteer counselors.

PURPOSE: To train and equip laypersons to provide free, biblically-based, confidential counsel to assist families and individuals in addressing financial questions or difficulties.

CONTENTS: This one-day, five-session workshop offers training for volunteers to become Good $ense budget counselors.

Train Everyone in Your Church

Good $ense Budget Course

FOR: Everyone in your church—not just those in financial difficulty.

PURPOSE: To train every believer to integrate Biblical Financial Principles into their lives—financially and spiritually.

CONTENTS: Contrasts the Pull of the Culture with the Mind and Heart of God in five areas—earning, giving, saving, spending, debt. Six, fifty-minute sessions can be taught in a variety of formats.

BESTSELLING WILLOW CREEK RESOURCES

Experience the Reality of God's Presence Every Day

An Ordinary Day with Jesus

JOHN ORTBERG AND RUTH HALEY BARTON

An Ordinary Day with Jesus uses aspects of an ordinary day and illustrates how we can connect with Jesus in those moments. Participants will learn how to:
- wake up and go to sleep in Jesus' name
- review their day with God
- silence competing voices in order to hear God's leadings
- experience time alone with God as an opportunity not an obligation
- use their own unique spiritual pathway to connect with God
- eliminate hurry and simplify their pace of life
- and much more!

	WCA ISBNs	Zondervan ISBNs
Leader's Guide	0744137217	0310245850
Participant's Guide	0744137225	0310245869
Drama Vignettes Video	0744136652	0310245575
PowerPoint CD-ROM	0744137195	0310245885
Complete Kit	0744136555	0310245877

*Link People and Their Gifts
with Ministries and Their Needs*

Network

Bruce Bugbee, Don Cousins, Bill Hybels

This proven, easy-to-use curriculum helps participants to discover their unique spiritual gifts, areas of passion for service, and individual ministry style.

Network helps believers better understand who God made them to be, and mobilizes them into meaningful service in the local church.

Using *Network*, your whole church can share a vision for each member and understand the vital role each plays in building God's Kingdom.

Leader's Guide	0310412412
Participant's Guide	0310412315
Drama Vignettes Video	0310411890
Overhead Masters	0310485282
Consultant's Guide	0310412218
Vision/Consultant Training Video	0310244994
Implementation Guide	0310432618
Complete Kit	0310212790

BESTSELLING WILLOW CREEK RESOURCES

Train Believers to Share Christ Naturally

Becoming a Contagious Christian

Mark Mittelberg, Lee Strobel, Bill Hybels

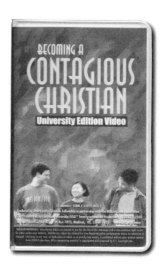

Over 500,000 believers have been trained to share their faith confidently and effectively with this proven curriculum. In eight, fifty-minute sessions, participants experience the joy of discovering their own unique evangelism style, learn how to transition conversations to spiritual topics, present gospel illustrations, and more.

Leader's Guide	0310500818
Participant's Guide	0310501016
Drama Vignettes Video	0310201691
Overhead Masters	0310500915
Complete Kit	0310501091

Also available—*Becoming a Contagious Christian* University Edition Video. Developed in partnership with InterVarsity Christian Fellowship, these drama vignettes feature college students building relationships with seekers. Designed to be used with the adult version of the curriculum.

Video	1558920412

Equip Students to Lead this Generation to Christ

Becoming a Contagious Christian Youth Edition

Mark Mittelberg, Lee Strobel, Bill Hybels

Revised and expanded for students by Bo Boshers

The award-winning *Becoming a Contagious Christian* curriculum has been revised and expanded to equip junior high and high school students to be contagious with their faith.

In eight, fifty-minute sessions, students learn how to:
- Develop relationships intentionally
- Transition an ordinary conversation to a spiritual conversation
- Tell their personal story of meeting Christ
- Share the gospel message using two different illustrations
- Answer ten common objections to Christianity
- Pray with a friend to receive Christ

Real stories of students who have led their friends to Christ make the material come alive as students see how God can work through them.

Leader's Guide	0310237718
Student's Guide	0310237734
Drama Vignettes Video	0310237742
Complete Kit	0310237696

BESTSELLING WILLOW CREEK RESOURCES

Bestselling Books by John Ortberg

If You Want to Walk on Water, You've Got to Get Out of the Boat

With engaging illustrations, humor, and relevant applications, John Ortberg explains how discerning God's call, rising above fear, and taking next steps can strengthen your faith.

Hardcover   0310228638

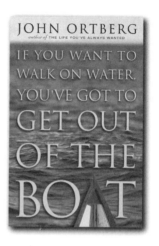

The Life You've Always Wanted

Gain a fresh perspective on the power of spiritual disciplines and how God can use them to deepen your relationship with him.

Hardcover   0310212146
Softcover   0310226996

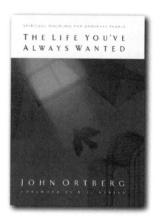

Love Beyond Reason

Filled with poignant illustrations, real-life applications, and humor, *Love Beyond Reason* describes the numerous facets of God's reason-defying, passionate love.

Hardcover   0310212154
Softcover   0310234492

Life-changing Small Group Resources

Pursuing Spiritual Transformation Series

John Ortberg, Laurie Pederson, Judson Poling

Explore fresh, biblically-based ways to think about and experience life with God through Willow Creek's Five Gs: Grace, Growth, Groups, Gifts, and Good Stewardship (Giving). Each study challenges the popular notion that merely "trying harder" will lead to Christlikeness. Instead, this series helps you identify the practices, experiences, and relationships God can use to help you become the person he longs for you to be.

Fully Devoted	0310220734
Grace	0310220742
Growth	0310220750
Groups	0310220769
Gifts	0310220777
Giving	0310220785

New Community Series

Bill Hybels, John Ortberg

New Community studies provide in-depth Bible study, thought-provoking questions, and community building exercises so groups can grow in faith together.

1 John: Love Each Other	0310227682
1 Peter: Stand Strong	0310227739
Acts: Build Community	0310227704
Colossians: Discover the New You	0310227690
Exodus: Journey Toward God	0310227712
James: Live Wisely	0310227674
Philippians: Run the Race	0310233143
Romans: Find Freedom	0310227658
Parables: Imagine Life God's Way	0310228816
Revelation: Experience God's Power	0310228824
Sermon on the Mount, part 1: Connect with God	0310228832
Sermon on the Mount, part 2: Connect with Others	0310228840

BESTSELLING WILLOW CREEK RESOURCES

Bible 101 Series

Bill Donahue, Kathy Dice, Judson Poling, Michael Redding, Gerry Mathisen

Bible 101 provides a solid, foundational understanding of God's Word in a format uniquely designed for a small group setting.

Cover to Cover	0830820639
Foundations	0830820612
Great Themes	0830820671
Interpretation	0830820655
Parables and Prophecy	0830820663
Personal Devotion	083082068X
Study Methods	0830820647
Times and Places	0830820620

InterActions Series

Bill Hybels

InterActions studies encourage participants to share interests, experiences, values, and lifestyles, and uses this common ground to foster honest communication, deeper relationships, and growing intimacy with God.

Authenticity	031020674X
Community	0310206774
Lessons in Love	0310206804
Marriage	0310206758
The Real You	0310206820
Commitment	0310206839
Essential Christianity	0310224438
Evangelism	0310206782
Freedom	0310217172
Getting a Grip	0310224446
Parenthood	0310206766
Serving Lessons	0310224462
Overcoming	0310224454
Character	0310217164
Fruits of the Spirit	0310213150
Jesus	0310213169
Prayer	0310217148
Psalms	0310213185
Transparency	0310217156
Transformation	0310213177

Walking with God Series

Don Cousins, Judson Poling

Practical, interactive, and biblically based, this dynamic series follows a two-track approach. Series 1 plugs new believers into the transforming power of discipleship to Christ. Series 2 guides mature believers into a closer look at the church.

Series 1
"Follow Me"	0310591635
Friendship with God	0310591430
The Incomparable Jesus	0310591538
Leader's Guide	0310592038

Series 2
Building Your Church	031059183X
Discovering Your Church	0310591732
Impacting Your World	0310591937
Leader's Guide	0310592135

Tough Questions Series

Garry Poole, Judson Poling

Created for seeker small groups, this series guides participants through an exploration of key questions about and objections to Christianity.

How Does Anyone Know God Exists?	0310222257
Is Jesus the Only Way?	0310222311
How Reliable Is the Bible?	0310222265
How Could God Allow Suffering/Evil?	0310222273
Don't All Religions Lead to God?	031022229X
Do Science and the Bible Conflict?	031022232X
Why Become a Christian?	0310222281
Leader's Guide	0310222249

BESTSELLING WILLOW CREEK RESOURCES

Build a Church Where Nobody Stands Alone

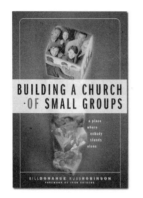

Building a Church of Small Groups
Bill Donahue, Russ Robinson

Experience the vision, values, and necessary initial steps to begin transitioning your church from a church *with* small groups to a church *of* small groups in this groundbreaking book.
Hardcover   0310240352

The Connecting Church
Randy Frazee

Pastor Randy Frazee explores the three essential elements of connecting churches: Common Purpose, Common Place, and Common Possessions. An excellent resource to help leaders create the kind of church where every member feels a deep sense of connection.
Hardcover   0310233089

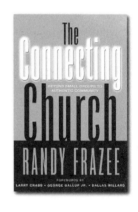

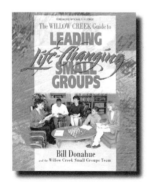

Leading Life-Changing Small Groups
Bill Donahue

Leading Life-Changing Small Groups covers everything from starting, structuring, leading, and directing an effective small group, to developing effective leaders.
Softcover   0310205956

The Coaches Handbook
This comprehensive resource provides teaching and tools to those who coach small group leaders. An excellent resource for small group ministry leaders.
Softcover   0744106567

Evangelistic Resources—for Believers and Seekers

Building a Contagious Church
Mark Mittelberg with contributions from Bill Hybels

Building a Contagious Church offers a proven, six-stage process to help your church become evangelistically contagious.
Hardcover   0310221498

Becoming a Contagious Christian
Bill Hybels and Mark Mittelberg

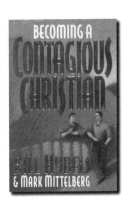

This groundbreaking book offers practical insights and real-life applications on how to reach friends and family for Christ.
Softcover   0310210089
Hardcover   0310485002

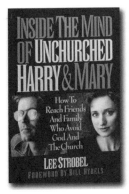

Inside the Mind of Unchurched Harry and Mary
Lee Strobel

Learn how to build relational bridges with friends and family who avoid God and the church.
Softcover   0310375614

The Case for Christ
Lee Strobel

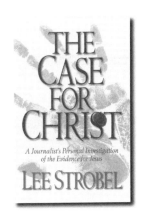

Award-winning investigative reporter Lee Strobel puts the toughest questions about Christ to acclaimed psychology, law, medicine, and biblical studies experts.
Softcover   0310209307

BESTSELLING WILLOW CREEK RESOURCES

The Case for Christ Student Edition

Lee Strobel with Jane Vogel

Based on the best-selling book for adults, the student edition is a fast, fun, informative tour through the evidence for Christ designed especially for students.
Softcover   0310234840

The Case for Faith

Lee Strobel

Tackles eight obstacles to faith, such as suffering, the doctrine of hell, evolution, and more.
Softcover   0310234697

The Journey

Uniquely designed to help spiritual seekers discover the relevance of Christianity.
Softcover   031092023X

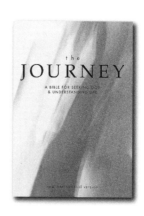

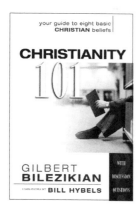

Christianity 101

Gilbert Bilezikian

Explores eight core beliefs of the Christian faith. A great resource for both seekers and believers.
Softcover   0310577012

WWW.WILLOWCREEK.COM

Proven Resources for Church Leaders

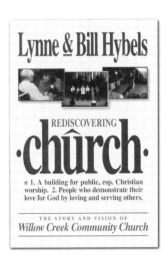

Rediscovering Church

Lynne and Bill Hybels

Rediscovering Church relates the beginnings of Willow Creek Community Church as well as its joys and struggles, and the philosophy and strategies behind its growth.
Softcover   0310219272

Leadership by the Book

Ken Blanchard, Bill Hybels, Phil Hodges

Filled with insights and simple strategies for becoming a successful leader, this best-selling book outlines the story of a professor and a pastor who mentor a young professional in management skills and ethics.
Hardcover   1578563089

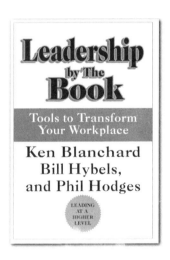

Casting a Courageous Vision

Bill Hybels, John Maxwell

In this inspiring video, Bill Hybels challenges those who attend Willow Creek to become active participants in fulfilling the mission God has for them. John Maxwell then shares principles to help you cast a compelling vision for your church.
Video   0310676045

BESTSELLING WILLOW CREEK RESOURCES

An Inside Look at the Willow Creek Worship Service

Featuring John Ortberg

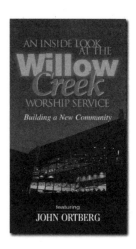

Experience Willow Creek's weekly worship service, New Community. Featured is a look at Willow Creek's worship style with patterns and ideas that can be integrated into your church's unique worship style.
Video   0310223571

The Heart of the Artist

Rory Noland

Willow Creek's music director looks at the unique gifts and challenges artists bring to spiritual life.
Softcover   0310224713

Drama Ministry

Steve Pederson

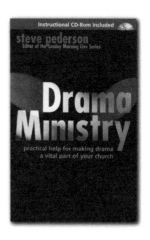

A powerful and practical "how-to" book for drama directors from the director of Willow Creek's drama ministry.
Softcover   0310219450

The Source

Scott Dyer and Nancy Beach

Whatever the size of your church, this book will help you and your staff plan creative, impactful services.
Softcover   0310500214